The Book of

WARFARE
WEAPONS
50 Advanced Spiritual Weapons For Christians

EZEKIEL WILLIAMS

The Book of

WARFARE
WEAPONS

50 Advanced Spiritual Weapons For Christians

H.C.STONE
ROCK SOLID PUBLISHING

WWW.HCSTONEPUBLISHING.COM

Published by

H C Stone Publishing, LLC

www.hcstonepublishing.com

EMAIL: hcstonepublishing@gmail.com

Printed in the United States of America

First Edition: July 2022

This book provides accurate and authoritative information concerning the subject matter covered. This information is given with the understanding that neither the author nor HC Stone Publishing, LLC is engaged in rendering professional legal advice.
Since the details of your situation are fact-dependent, you should additionally seek the services of a competent professional. The publisher is not responsible for websites (or their content) that are not owned by the publisher.

To my best friend, better-half,
lover of my life, and beautiful wife:

Janice Fernandez Williams

I prayed to God that He would bless me with a wife
who possessed three essential traits. God said, *"No.
Take a pen and paper and write down these 86 traits."*
He sent you to me with all 86 traits when I would have settled
for only 3.

Wow! You have blessed my life beyond measure.

Thank you for your love, support, understanding, and for being
the embodiment of the proverbial virtuous woman.
Thank you for your dedication, authenticity, joy, and for bringing back
laughter when it was away on a lengthy vacation.
Thank you for your unwavering faith and for believing in our dream.
I am so happy that we are taking this journey
of life together as we become one.
I thank God for you every day.
I love you—forever

"And the Lord shall utter his voice before his army: for his camp is very great: for he is strong and executeth his word: for the day of the Lord is great and very terrible; and who can abide it?" (Joel 2:11)

CONTENTS

CONTENTS

CONTENTS

CONTENTS

PREFACE

The Book of Warfare Weapons is the second book in *The Book of Warfare Series.* The purpose of this book is to help motivate, train, and equip Christians to triumph in spiritual warfare by effectively using 50 different spiritual weapons.

Throughout my journey of writing this book, I have discovered that many Christians lack proper training in how to wage effective spiritual combat. Many often search the Internet looking for solutions to their most urgent challenges in life. They often come across new fads, modern philosophies, and popular humanistic reasoning that may sound good at the time but fail to deliver when the storms of life arise.

They fail to take into account that real spiritual entities of darkness are constantly fighting to destroy the souls of mankind. These are evil beings that are immune to humanistic reasoning and ideologies. They only respond to authority and power. Ultimate authority and power come from Jesus Christ. Jesus gave Christians power and authority over all the powers of darkness.

A person may have authority and power and not know how to use them. The result of which is a person who is ineffective, incompetent, and headed toward defeat. Take, for instance, a police officer trying to carry out his daily duties without a weapon. Thugs will not only disrespect him, but they may even attempt to harm him because he is ill-equipped without his weapon.

Likewise, in the spirit realm, evil entities will disrespect, harass, bully, and even attempt to harm Christians who do not have or know how to use their spiritual weapons. Therefore, if training in the proper use of one's weapon is essential, how much more is training in all 50? Training in the appropriate use of 50 different spiritual weapons is a gigantic, life-altering phenomenon of grand proportions.

This book will train you to unleash weapons of unimaginable authority, power, and might. These weapons are older than time. These weapons proved themselves effective in dispensations and generations throughout the history of the human experience. These weapons can be activated anytime, anywhere, and in any situation.

For twenty-five years, the Holy Spirit began to take me behind the scenes of the spirit realm to teach me how to use these spiritual weapons. The Holy Spirit began to teach me by giving me countless visions, dreams, interpretations of dreams, prophecies, miracles, signs, and testimonies concerning these weapons.

Furthermore, through many tests, trials, tribulations, and persecutions, I have proven the enduring relevance of many of these weapons. God has used both the good times and the tough times to impart valuable lessons on how to win at spiritual warfare. First, the Lord instructed me to write the things He had shown me in my journal. Now, twenty-five journals later, the Lord has told me to turn my journals into books to help others.

It has been a long journey to bring this book to print. This book is unique because its viewpoint is practical rather than historical, philosophical, or theological. As a pastor and a prophet, God has allowed me to experience many spiritual revelations. This book can help you also to experience rock-solid, biblically based victory through Holy Spirit revelation.

All spiritual revelations and experiences should point to the finished work of Jesus Christ on the Cross and His work of grace in the lives of believers. God has given us mighty spiritual weapons, but we need the wisdom and revelation from the Holy Spirit to use them correctly and effectively.

All wisdom, revelations, or experiences from God will always center around our Lord Jesus Christ. Therefore, all revelations and spiritual experiences that do not align with or conflict with God's written Word must be rejected, for the Word of God is the ultimate authority in heaven, on earth, and under the earth.

It is my prayer that upon reading this book, your faith will grow to new heights, and your confidence in God will soar. Get ready to become an effective, victorious, spiritual-armed warrior as you start your training through *The Book of Warfare Weapons*!

Thank you, and God bless.   – Prophet Ezekiel Williams

ACKNOWLEDGEMENTS

Thank you, Heavenly Father, for your perfect love. Thank you, Lord Jesus, for your saving Grace. Thank you, Holy Spirit, for your abiding presence.

To my mom, Evangelist Alfredia Williams: thank you for being my inspiration, my role model, my teacher, my spiritual counselor, my closest friend, and my heart. Thank you for giving me a happy childhood, a loving home, and for teaching me as a child about Jesus Christ. I love, adore you, and appreciate you.

To my spiritual covering, role model, mentor, and friend, Bishop Henry Fernandez (Pastor Carol Fernandez and boys): thank you for all you have done for me. You have greatly impacted my life. I have been transformed under your anointed ministry at The Faith Center. I love you, appreciate you, and thank you.

To my incredible wife, Janice, whom I love, as Christ loves the church: thank you for being the wonderful woman you are. You have helped me to believe that anything is indeed possible. Thank you for believing in me, supporting me, and encouraging me to go after every dream. You have inspired me beyond words. You are a true gift from God. I love you, cherish you, and appreciate you. I thank God for you.

To my daughters, Vannessa Williams and Gabryel Williams: thank you for being the best daughters a father could have. You have blossomed into beautiful, intelligent, caring, and accomplished young ladies. Thank you for years of laughter, kindness, understanding, and unconditional love. I love you, appreciate you, and I am so proud of both of you.

To Mother Thelma Fernandez: you are fantastic. I thank you for being a wonderful mother-in-law and a great person. You are a great example of faith, compassion, and goodness. I love you and thank God for you.

To Aunt Sharon: I cannot thank you enough for everything you have done for me and impacted my life. You are a divine blessing to everyone who has the great pleasure of knowing you. I love you and thank God for you.

To my brothers & sisters: Pastor Harry (Lady Gwen) Houston, Bro. Mathis (Sis. Minnie) Williams, Evangelists Julie (Bishop James) Hagan, Pastor Johnny (Lady Joy) Williams, Pastor James Williams, Missionary Alfredia (Dec. Nathaniel)

Golden, Bro. Paul Williams (Sis. Alveda), Minister Ann (Minister Eric) Russell, Bro. Archie (Sis. Merlin) Williams, Sis. Evon (Bro. Kenny) Roberts, Minister Timothy Williams, and Elder Earnest Williams (Minister Aletta): you are the best family ever. I love each of you.

To the Fernandez Family: Father-in-law, Pastor Regmond (Lady Karol); brothers-in-law Roderick, Duane, and nephew Nikolii, Mike and Faye, Clavel "Sharon," Joan, Judith, love each of you, and I thank God for you.

To the Williams, Fernandez, Houston, and Thompson Families: To all my uncles, aunts, cousins, nieces, nephews, and additional family members too numerous to name: I say you know that each of you are in my heart. I love each of you and thank God for you.

To The Faith Center Ministries International, TFC ministerial team, University of Fort Lauderdale (UFTL), TFC staff, all departments, ministries, and TFC ROC Ministries: Thank you. Let Jesus Christ continue to shine and love through you.

To all my friends, partners, and supporters of Tuesday World, Spiritual Warfare Bootcamps, APC Business Success Seminars, Prophetic Prayer Seminars, and the Book of Warfare series: thank you for your kindness, encouragement, and constant support.

Special Thanks to Angela Russell and Evon Roberts for editorial consulting; Doran for cover design. Sarah and Cristina for drawings. To my close friends, classmates, co-workers, and associates whose names are too numerous to mention: I say thank you, and God bless.

INTRODUCTION

Are you tired of being oppressed, held back, blocked, or restrained? Do you find yourself facing the same challenges as if you are in an unbroken cycle? Are you or your family battling addictions, bondages, or generational curses?

Do you experience continual sabotage of opportunities, promotions, and breakthroughs that you know belong to you? If any of these describes you, you have help in *The Book of Warfare Weapons*.

This book is packed with practical and proven strategies to help you succeed in spiritual warfare. These are some of the benefits you can expect to receive when you read this book.

You can expect to:
* receive a strategic plan for defeating the powers of darkness.
* experience tremendous transformation in your life.
* put to flight the armies of the evil one.
* see quicker answers to prayers.
* demolish bondages, yokes, and addictions.
* receive biblical solutions to problems in life.
* experience an increase in fruitfulness and abundance in life.
* develop a strong desire to pray.
* display a strong motivation for sharing your faith.

God desires that all people know His Word. However, many people are reluctant to embrace the Bible or Christianity because they don't understand it. They often get lost in all the Bible customs, church traditions, and religious ordinances. Religion often puts barriers in the way to hinder men from coming to Jesus. I wrote this book intending to remove many of those barriers while keeping you connected to the miracle-working power of God.

This book discusses biblical concepts that are hard to understand and attempts to explain them in a clear and simplified manner. While simplification is the goal, it in no wise implies watered-down, elementary, or superficial. On the contrary, this book is potent, with advanced wisdom that reaches the heart of all human experiences.

In this book, you will encounter an easy-to-learn spiritual warfare-weapons training program. If you commit to completing the program step-by-step, I can assure you that the mighty power of God will forever transform you.

This book should bring you hours of memorable experiences and enjoyable victories. It will arm you with powerful weapons to rout all the works of darkness. It will challenge you to go after your dreams and to fulfill God's will for your life.

And it will fill you with renewed hope and strength, reminding you that your destiny is in God's hands. And with faith, you can enjoy a triumphant present and a successful future.

Many people have proven the principles of this book to be both effective and reliable. In addition, numerous individuals have had the opportunity to participate in our Spiritual Warfare Boot Camp program. As a result, they have received first-hand training and mentoring in `using these spiritual weapons. As a result, the testimonies continue to pour in, attesting to the proven wisdom of God's Word and the effective weaponry revealed within this book.

I care deeply about your spiritual success. I want to help you reach every dream that you have set for yourself in life. I desire to share with you wondrous things that can assist you in your journey toward victory. I believe this book will help equip and empower you to do so.

Like you, I have some regrets in life. I can genuinely say, "If only I knew then what I know now." I wish I had this book when I was younger, for I would have made far fewer mistakes in life. This book can help you experience tremendous successes that are too numerous to list.

While I cannot change the past, I am so grateful for the present and excited about a glorious future, for this book has helped me connect to the power of God in a real and practical way. This book is not a substitute for the Bible. It is a tool to help you better study and appreciate your Bible.

Remember, the Bible says, "For though we walk in the flesh, we do not war after the flesh: (For the weapons of our warfare are not carnal, but mighty through God to the pulling down of strongholds;) Casting down imaginations, and every high thing that exalteth itself against the

knowledge of God, and bringing into captivity every thought to the obedience of Christ" (2 Corinthians 10:3-5).

This book provides the opportunity that you have been waiting for to advance in spiritual warfare. In this book, you will discover divine secrets that will change your life forever. Reading this book will teach you to exercise spiritual weapons that are older than time, faster than light, and stronger than death. Imagine yourself having a ready set of solutions for every challenge that you will ever experience in life.

Now, imagine yourself using them to such an extent that nothing becomes impossible for you ever again. You will be able to exercise mighty weapons that have the power to change everything concerning you, your family, your community, and the world. Thus, you will be able to advance the Kingdom of God in a great and mighty way.

If you are ready to start pulling down strongholds, imaginations, and high things exalted against the knowledge of God, then this book is for you. If you are prepared to harass the enemy that once harassed you, this book is for you. If you are ready to start taking ground and walking in dominion, this book is for you.

This book will help to level both the playing field and the battlefield of life. It will show you how to use your spiritual weapons—weapons given to you by God, of which you may not have known that you had.

This book will become a catalyst to help you experience a change in levels, a change in seasons, and a change in your destiny. It will help to rewrite your life story to one of victory by faith.

If you are ready to rise like a mighty-armed warrior for Christ, turn the page and begin now.

viii

THE DREAM: Spirits Can Feel Pain

They were about 3-feet tall and had big-bulging eyes that looked too big for their heads. They looked as if they were made of a substance of the likeness of animal fur and, at times, the similarity of vapors of black smoke. They stood upright like humans and were intelligent to the point they could talk and reason

I heard them laugh, but it was no regular laugh, nor did it come from a heart of joy. Instead, their laughter came from a deep place of darkness. They laughed as they recanted how they inflicted pain and suffering on many unsuspecting souls. It was a nervous and spooky laugh, as if they could not control it.

I watched them as the wind blew them into a house. They passed through the solid wall of the house as if it was never there. Then, a breeze blew them to the bedside of a man who was fast asleep. I asked, "Lord, what are they doing there?" He said, "Watch." I saw as the eyes of the two demons grew bigger with excitement and amazement! They were amazed at the opportunity that presented itself. I thought to myself, *What opportunity could that be?*

Then, the second demon answered the first demon as if a question was asked without words. The second demon responded, "You know that it is forbidden!" The first demon replied, "Yeah, but look at him. How often do we get a chance like this?! They both laughed nervously, and then they simultaneously lunged at the sleeping man.

What I witnessed next I will never forget. The two demons jumped on the man and began to punch him as many times as they could in rapid succession. Each time they hit him, a bump, bruise, or blister would arise on the man. They continually and nervously looked around the room as if to watch so that they would not get caught.

Sometimes when they would hit, the man, his body, would shake from the punch. I thought to myself, *Why doesn't he do something?* There were a couple of times it looked as if he was going to wake up from his slumber, but instead, he would turn over, reposition himself in bed, and continue sleeping.

I wanted to do something to help the man. I saw the bruises, bumps, and blisters that the demons gave him. I saw him turn back and forth in his bed as if he was in a deep sleep from which he could not wake up. The assault seemed to go on for a long time because they were hitting him so fast, but it was only about 30 seconds of human time.

I said, "Lord, make them stop!" He said, "Watch." Then, finally, the man had enough. While still in his state of sleep, he mustered enough strength to whisper "Jesus," and before the word could fully come out of his mouth, power hit that room.

It came faster than lightning, and while the Name "Jesus" was still rolling off his tongue, there appeared a mighty angel in the room, restraining the arms of the demons with a crushing, tight, vice-grip manner of holding. The angel moved faster than lightning. He moved so quickly that it shocked the demons, for he appeared amid them before they could even blink.

The angel said not one word, nor did he move again from the first moment that he grabbed their arms. He just stood still as a mighty servant of the Almighty God, in power and strength. He did not look at the demons at all. But with great care and concern, he looked at the battered and bruised man who was still sleeping in his bed.

I thought to myself. *That's it??? That's all he had to do was call on the name "Jesus?!" He had the power to stop the assault when it first began?!! Why didn't he stop it before now?!!* I was beyond shocked. [NOTE: In addition to calling on the Name of Jesus, praying before going to bed could have also prevented those demons from being able to harass him].

I had lots of questions for the Lord. I wanted to ask the Lord, "Why did you allow this? Why did it take the man so long to stop it? Where was the angel in the beginning?" Before I could receive an answer, I saw something else that amazed me.

I witnessed as the power of Jesus began to heal the battered and bruised man as he continued to sleep. I saw as all the bruises, bumps, and blisters grew smaller and smaller until they disappeared completely. The man was healed entirely by Jesus only after about a minute of the angel's arrival on the scene. I was amazed by what I saw and heard. In addition, I perceived that most people experiencing similar encounters would think that they only had a bad dream or would not remember their dream at all.

Then there was yelling, screaming, and cries of deep anguish and pain from the demons. I thought, *Why are they making so much noise?* Then, again, the Lord said, "Watch." I watched as the demons tried with all their strength, power, and might to remove their arms from the vice-like grip of the angel, but to no avail.

They could not budge it. There was so much power and strength in the mighty angel that merely clinched their arms when restraining them was causing them excruciating pain as they cried out in anguish. They pleaded with him to let them go, but he did not respond to them; he only held them fast.

At that moment, I received revelation from the Lord that "Spirits can

feel pain!!!" The dream ended, but that revelation forever changed my understanding of spiritual warfare. The evil spirits that once harassed, antagonized, and troubled me can all feel pain.

Jesus Christ gave us power and authority over all the power of the devil. I can do something to turn the tables in my favor. I can cause pain to the very entities that once caused me emotional, financial, and physical pain throughout my life. This revelation that spirits can feel pain is an empowering truth.

According to the Bible, as recorded in the book of Matthew, chapter 8, demons can feel pain. We read how Jesus went to a county to rescue a man possessed with many demons. As Jesus got closer, the demons cried out to God to help save them from Jesus. The demons cried out in fear, asking Jesus if He had come to torment them before their time (Matthew 8:29).

Demons and devils all know that there is an appointed time that they will experience excruciating pain and extreme torment forever in the Lake of Fire (Matthew 25:41; Revelation 21:8; and Revelation 20:10). The devil doesn't want you to realize that he is helpless to avoid God's wrath. The devil doesn't want you to see that he is a defeated, doomed, and damned spirit. Therefore, in every generation, he has gone to great lengths to hide the reality of his impending doom.

You would be surprised to know the number of people (including some misinformed Christians) who believe the following: 1) Satan is immune to fire; 2) Satan is in Hell; 3) Satan don't have a body; therefore, he can't be burned or experience pain. How many times have you seen a drawing or cartoon depicting Satan sitting on a throne in Hell, enjoying the fire while being immune to its effect?

These are all lies. Satan is a created being. The Almighty and all-wise God who created him (as a good angel before he sinned and became an evil angel) knows what causes Satan pleasure and what causes him pain. God in His wisdom created the Lake of Fire to punish Satan and his angels in eternal torment.

Jesus is the Eternal Victorious One! Satan is the forever defeated one! Jesus defeated Satan so many times that it is without number. Jesus defeated Lucifer, kicked him out of Heaven, and changed his name to Satan (the devil). Jesus defeated Satan at Noah's flood. Jesus defeated Satan at the Tower of Babel.

In addition, Jesus defeated Satan by coming to earth as a baby, born of a virgin. Jesus defeated Satan by dying on the Cross at Calvary. Jesus defeated Satan by rising from the dead. Jesus defeated Satan by ascending into Heaven and sitting at the right hand of God. Moreover, Jesus defeated Satan by sending the Holy Spirit. Also, Jesus defeated Satan by sending power to His believers (and giving them power over all the power of the enemy Acts 1:8 and Luke 10:19).

Furthermore, Satan experience daily defeats as believers receive continual testimonies of miracles, signs, and wonders through faith and prayer. Jesus will defeat him at the rapture, defeat him at the beginning of the Millennial reign of Christ, and defeat him at the battle of Armageddon. Finally, Jesus will ultimately defeat him at the Great White Throne Judgment when Jesus Christ will cast Satan into the Lake of Fire.

Because defeat is the devil's portion, it is not appointed to Satan to ever have victory over the children of God (by sheer authority, power, or might alone). For it is written, "Greater is He that is within you than he that is in the world." (1 John 4:4)

Satan, therefore, knows that he is no match for the sheer authority, power, and might that God allows to radiate through His children at any given point in time. Jesus said, "Behold, I give you the power to tread on serpents and scorpions, and overall the powers of the enemy." All means all!!! If God gives believers power over all the power of the enemy, that means there is no power of the enemy that saints do not have dominion over. Again, all means all.

Yet, children of God often misuse their power, authority, position, possessions, gifts, talents, and abilities to hand Satan unauthorized, temporary victories. They give him quick victories that he is not entitled to and ones he could not win by his own authority, power, or might.

Thus, ignorance of the Word of God is the primary cause of Christians suffering unnecessary setbacks, delays, disappointments, and defeats in life. Not because the enemy is so powerful or wise (for defeat is his portion), but because Christians often fail to exercise their New Covenant authority, power, wisdom, and weapons as revealed in the Word of God.

God said, "My people are destroyed daily for lack of knowledge" (Hosea 4:6). In other words, because you don't know the spiritual laws of Heaven, the enemy is using them against you. Satan is using your ignorance of the Word of God as a spiritual-legal technicality to rob, steal, kill, and destroy so much of what the Father has given you as a redeemed citizen of Heaven living on earth.

Therefore, you must know your Heavenly Constitution (called the Word of God) to enforce your privileges as a citizen of Heaven, your Authority as a Child of God, and your eternal purpose in Jesus Christ.

Jesus Christ's redemptive work at Calvary brought us into a new covenant based on better promises, benefits, and blessings than those found in the Old Testament Covenant. The benefits of the Old Testament gave the heroes of faith, authority, and power to reign on earth. So likewise, the benefits of the New Covenant provide us with authority and power to reign in Heaven and on earth (Matthew 16: 19: Ephesians 2:6; Revelation 3:21; and Matthew 18:18).

Our New Covenant position in Jesus Christ enables us to operate in higher authority, power, strength, spiritual fruits, spiritual gifts, and spiritual weapons than in the old covenant. The Holy Spirit empowers and teaches us all things about our new identity in Jesus Christ.

The purpose of this book is to share with you revelation and insight into how to use the 50 Spiritual Weapons God has given us in Jesus Christ. These weapons will help you enforce the enemy's defeat, advance the Kingdom of Heaven's agenda on earth, and help you implement your spiritual rights to reign in life by Jesus Christ (Romans 5:17).

As you learn of each weapon, put them into daily practice by activating strategies, tactics, and exercising activities found in this The Book of Warfare Weapon-Manual; The Book of Warfare Weapons-Workbook; and The Book of Warfare-Journal.

Now, let's get familiar with using the 50 spiritual weapons and how each can help you in your daily life and help you fulfill your destiny in Christ.

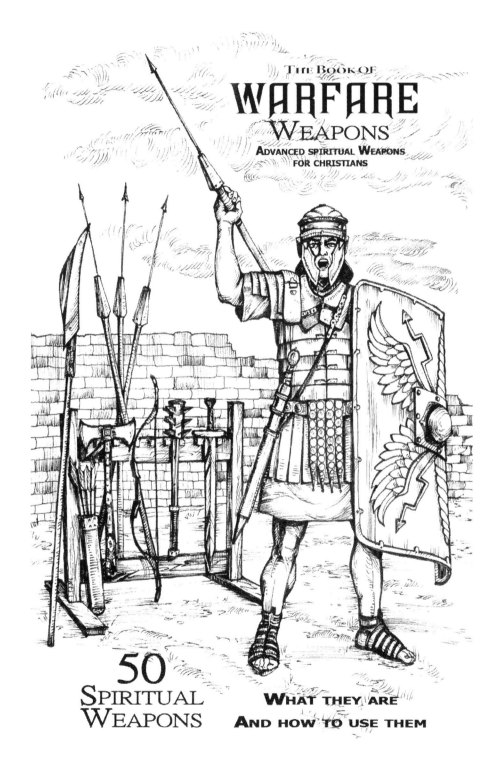

THE BOOK OF

WARFARE

WEAPONS

ADVANCED SPIRITUAL WEAPONS
FOR CHRISTIANS

50
SPIRITUAL
WEAPONS

WHAT THEY ARE
AND HOW TO USE THEM

SELECT YOUR LEVEL OF TRAINING
Complete the following challenges and activities to advance in levels.

1a) The Book of Warfare Weapons – Manual

1b) The Book of Warfare Weapons- Social Media Challenge

2) The Book of Warfare Weapons- Workbook

3) The Book of Warfare Weapons- Activities Journal

4) The Book of Warfare Weapons- 8-Hour Audio Training Kit

5) The Book of Warfare- Warriors Group Challenge

6) The Book of Warfare- Outstanding Warriors Challenge (TBOWW-OWC).

7) TBOWW Online Spiritual Warfare Boot Camp.

---

* NOVICE LEVEL-1 Complete activities 1a and 1b.

* BEGINNER LEVEL-2 Completes 1a, 1b, and 2.

* INTERMEDIATE LEVEL-3 Completes 1 through 3.

* JOURNEYMAN-LEVEL-4 Completes 1 through 4.

* ADVANCED LEVEL -5 Completes 1 through 5.

* WARRIOR LEVEL-6 Completes 1 through 6.

* ADVANCED WARRIOR LEVEL-7 Completes 1 to 7.

How To Best Use This Book

The Book of Warfare Weapons is a training manual for teaching about the 50 different spiritual weapons, their origins, their functions, their power, and how to effectively use each of them.

It is one part of a comprehensive training program that deals with many different aspects of Spiritual Warfare from a Christian perspective and a Biblical context. The goal is to help train and equipped you with knowledge of all 50 spiritual weapons so you can prosper in life. A person must be born again and Baptized in the Holy Spirit to effectively use them all continuously.

This book can be used as a stand-alone training manual, but you will experience the greatest transformation and maximum impact if you go through all seven levels of the training. Moreover, you can have greater and more unique experiences when you take the training with a small group of your family, dear relatives, near church members, and close friends.

When studying each lesson, picture yourself using the spiritual weapon in real-life situations and getting the results that are indicated in the Bible. Each spiritual weapon produces power for replication and duplication of stated victories. When you exercise each lesson take the time to find out what works better and what works best.

TBOWW Workbook and TBOWW Journal will help you to define and refine your approach, tactics, and strategies, presented in the manual. More in-depth teachings, revelation, visions, dreams, personal testimonies of miracles, signs, wonders, and life lessons can all be found in the 8-Hour Audio training kit.

Furthermore, when using this book always read your Bible to see what God's Word says about each of the spiritual weapons. Commit to a lifestyle of prayer and to be led by the Holy Spirit, in the Name of the Lord Jesus Christ. The more you exercise in each of them the more prepared you will be when facing your day of battle.

TBOW

OUTSTANDING WARRIORS CHALLENGE

RAISING WARRIORS TO WIN

The Book of Warfare Weapons
Chapter 1
Prayer of Agreement

Primary Purpose: To increase the strength of faith
Effective Use: Enables one to resist a troop
Strength: Very strong

Scripture:
"Again, I say unto you, that if two of you shall agree on earth as touching any thing that they shall ask, it shall be done for them of my Father which is in heaven" (Matthew 18:19).

The Attack: You believe God for something, but the enemy is opposing you with lies, doubts, and unbelief to undermine your faith. You think, "If only I had someone to stand with me in faith concerning this matter, things would be different."

Weapon of Choice: The Prayer of Agreement.
Defensively: This weapon is effective against being overwhelmed, outnumbered, isolated, lonely, loss of hope, and having a doubtful heart.
Offensively: This weapon helps to strengthen the faith of the petitioner and helps to accelerate the manifestation of prayer requests.

Important Notes for this Weapon: Make sure that the person you agree with in prayer is saved, has faith, and feels a strong desire to see you prosper in life.

How to Use this Weapon: Ask the person to agree with you in faith, believing God, to answer your prayer request. Tell the person your request to see if you both are in agreement. If the person is willing, and you both agree, then both of you can pray together, believing that the answer shall manifest.

Secrets of this Weapon: In the spirit realm, it is as if you are calling for backup that will accompany your faith. Your faith, added to their faith, results in a multiplication of faith. The Bible tells us that one can chase a thousand, and two can put ten thousand to flight (Deuteronomy 32:30). The more people you can get to agree with you in faith and prayer, the greater the power that will be released concerning your request.

The Book of Warfare Weapons
Chapter 1
Prayer of Agreement

Weapon's Source of Power: The divine unity of God powers this amazing weapon. Christ is in God, God is in Christ, and we are in Him (John 17:21-23). We affirm this divine truth and release a measure of its power each time we pray the Prayer of Agreement.

Faith Heroes Using this Weapon: Hannah (1 Samuel 1:12-18); Manoah and his wife (Judges 13:8-16); Paul (2 Thessalonians 3:1-2); Apostle Peter (Acts 12:5); and many others.

PICK YOUR CHALLENGE: For a more immersive experience pick your challenge below and complete it according to the instructions listed. For the best experience and maximum impact complete all activities, exercises, and challenges.

Your Challenge: Begin to pray the Prayer of Agreement as often as you like to accelerate the manifestation of all your prayer requests.

For A Great Challenge: Complete activities in Chapter #1 of *The Book of Warfare Weapons–Workbook.*

For A Group Challenge: Complete the Group Challenge of Chapter #1 of *The Book of Warfare Weapons–Workbook.*

For A Great Online Challenge: Complete the online activities and challenges in Chapter #1 of *The Book of Warfare Weapons–Outstanding Warrior Challenge (TBOWW-OWC) online challenge at* www.tbowowc.com.

The Book of Warfare Weapons
Chapter 1
Prayer of Agreement

Prayer of Activation: (*Hold hands with the person you agree with as a point of contact. Then, pray this prayer:*) Heavenly Father, thank You for allowing us to come into Your presence. We come before You in obedience to Your Holy Word according to _____ (*find a Bible verse showing God's promise*) which says _____ (*say or read the scripture verse you are claiming*). As legal beneficiaries of the new covenant of redemption, we touch and agree together in faith, believing for the following prayer request: (*now pray the request_____*). (*While one is praying, the other person is listening, praying, and agreeing in faith for all the person has requested from God*). We thank You, Father, that we now receive the answer to our prayer. In the Name of Jesus Christ, we pray. Amen.

The Book of Warfare Weapons
Chapter 2
Binding and Loosing

Primary Purpose: To deny or approve works in your life
Effective Use: Spiritual opposition
Strength: Unlimited power

Scriptures:

"And I will give unto thee the keys of the kingdom of heaven: and whatsoever thou shalt bind on earth shall be bound in heaven; and whatsoever thou shalt loose on earth shall be loosed in heaven" (Matthew 16:19).

"Verily I say unto you, Whatsoever ye shall bind on earth shall be bound in heaven: and whatsoever ye shall loose on earth shall be loosed in heaven" (Matthew 18:18).

The Attack: You realize that all your efforts keep coming up short and ending in failure. Your desires and expectations often result in disappointment, and you wonder why. You can only get to a certain point in life before hitting a wall—you can go no further. You labor for a harvest, but you never get a chance to reap its rewards.

Weapon of Choice: Binding and Loosing.

Defensively: These weapons are great for canceling out evil plans, attacks, and opposition from the enemy. These weapons are effective against stagnation, oppression, suppression, poverty, wickedness, curses, bondages, addictions, chaos, and confusion.

Offensively: These weapons are great for approving blessings, favor, mercy, and the goodness of God to have complete liberty in your life.

Important Notes for this Weapon: Jesus gave all believers spiritual authority and power. Like police officers who have power and authority on earth to stop, block, arrest, and restrain evil, so do we. As saints of God, we have even greater power and authority through Jesus to overcome the forces of darkness. God has given us power and authority on the earth so that whatever work we approve or "loose" may continue. Whatever work we deny or "bind," it must stop. Each believer has the individual responsibility to "bind" evil works and "loose" good works on the earth.

4

The Book of Warfare Weapons
Chapter 2
Prayer of Binding and Loosing

Also, never bind a human being, for that is witchcraft. Our fight is not with human beings but with evil spirits that use and control them. Jesus Christ came not to bind men but for all bound men (captives) to be free.

How to Use this Weapon: Be strategic by using a prayer list. While in prayer, begin to bind (and loose) all the things on your prayer list. You do this by "binding" the enemy's assignments, schemes, and operations from being carried out against you (and others) on the earth. In the same manner, you should approve the holy angels of God to work on your behalf on the earth, according to the Word of God. You do this by "loosing" the angels of God to go forth and to usher to you every good and pleasant success on the earth according to the Father's will.

Secrets of this Weapon: In the spirit realm, it is like you've received a court order from the Supreme Court of Heaven that denies what you deny and approves what you approve. The Heavenly Court is ruled by King Jesus, who is King of Kings and Lord of Lords.

Weapon's Source of Power: Jesus is the Almighty Creator and rightful Owner of all things in Heaven and on earth. It is God's divine right to give power and authority over His possessions to anyone whom He chooses. Jesus chose to give this power to His believers (Matthew 16:19). The delegated power of divine ownership is released each time this weapon is activated.

Faith Heroes Using this Weapon: Elijah (James 5:17-18); Elisha (2 Kings 6:17–loosing, verse 18–binding, verse 20–loosing); Peter (Acts 5:9-11); Paul (Acts 13:11); and many others.

PICK YOUR CHALLENGE: For a more immersive experience pick your challenge below and complete it according to the instructions listed.
For the best experience and maximum impact complete all activities, exercises, and challenges.

The Book of Warfare Weapons
Chapter 2
Prayer of Binding and Loosing

Your Challenge: Take a few moments to consider all the things happening in your life right now. Are there some negative things that you are allowing in your life that you should bind? Are good things being restrained from you that you should be loosing?

For A Great Challenge: Complete activities in Chapter #2 of *The Book of Warfare Weapons–Workbook*.

For A Group Challenge: Complete the Group Challenge of Chapter #2 of *The Book of Warfare Weapons–Workbook*.

For A Great Online Challenge: Complete the online activities and challenges in Chapter #2 of *The Book of Warfare Weapons–Outstanding Warrior Challenge (TBOWW-OWC) online challenge at* <u>www.tbowowc.com</u>.

Prayer of Activation: Father, I come by way of the Blood of Jesus. Thank You for dying on the cross to destroy sin and for rising from the grave to give me eternal life. Thank You for ascending into Heaven and giving me power on earth to bind and to loose. Therefore, in accordance with Your Word as recorded in Matthew 16:19, I bind all forces of darkness (*all bad and negative things in your life*) that are operating against me on the earth (*list them and declare them out loud*). In the Name of Jesus Christ, I cancel out all operations and assignments sent against me in the area of (state the area(s) here_____). I bind these things that are opposing me on the earth in the Name of Jesus Christ. I declare all opposing works of darkness to be null and void. I loose on the earth and declare (*all good and positive things that relate to life and Godliness*) to be free to work in my life (*list them and declare them out loud*). I believe by faith that it is so now. I thank You for it, Father. In the Name of Jesus Christ, I pray. Amen.

The Book of Warfare Weapons
Chapter 3
Prayer of Consecration

Primary Purpose: To increase intimacy with God
Effective Use: Stagnation and restriction
Strength: Very strong

Scriptures:

"And he was withdrawn from them about a stone's cast, and kneeled, and prayed. Saying, *Father, if thou be willing, remove this cup from me: nevertheless, not my will, but thine, be done*" (Luke 22:41-42).

"I delight to do thy will, O my God: yea, thy law is within my heart" (Psalm 40:8). "And who then is willing to consecrate himself this day to the LORD?" (1 Chronicles 29:5b).

The Attack: You are saved and love God, but don't spend personal time with Him. You only read your Bible at Church or pray when you need something. You are too busy with the cares of life to do God's will. You are not sure of your God-given purpose and whether you are fulfilling it or not. You feel spiritually stagnant and need spiritual refreshing from the Lord.

Weapon of Choice: The Prayer of Consecration.

Defensively: This weapon is effective against pride, arrogance, selfishness, self-righteousness, procrastination, emptiness, dryness, fruitlessness, carnality, laziness, foolishness, stubbornness, disobedience, and rebellion.

Offensively: This is an effective weapon that can draw you closer to God. It helps to create intimacy between you and God. It is excellent for increasing the measure of anointing and power that rests upon your life and flows through your life. Also, it increases your obedience to God.

Important Notes for this Weapon: When God saves a person, the person must still surrender their will to God continually. God never takes away a person's will, but God will accept the person's will if they freely submit it to Him. When it comes to being used by God, a person must die to their own will. Consecration is the term used when one is intentionally laying down their will to accept God's will.

The Book of Warfare Weapons
Chapter 3
Prayer of Consecration

It is also the availing of oneself to be reserved entirely for God. In other words, you are zealous, in a good way, to become God's very best friend because you love Him.

How to Use this Weapon: Set aside a specific amount of time to read your Bible, pray, worship, meditate on Jesus, and fellowship with God without distractions. Focus on surrendering your complete will to God. Focus on developing intimacy with God as only a close friend can. Ask the Holy Spirit to help you experience faithful fellowship with God and make spending time with Him your top priority.

Secrets of this Weapon: The heart of God, manifested in the heart of the believer, is the secret to this powerful weapon.

Weapon's Source of Power: The obedient life of Jesus Christ energizes this weapon. Jesus loved God with all His heart (Matthew 22:37). Because Jesus loved God, He devoted Himself to living a consecrated life of complete obedience unto His Heavenly Father. Jesus was so obedient that He was willing to die rather than disobey His Father. Jesus defeated death when God raised Jesus from the dead through the power of the Holy Spirit. We receive power from the life of Jesus Christ when we consecrate ourselves in obedience to doing the Father's will from a willing heart.

Faith Heroes Using this Weapon: Jacob (Genesis 28:20-22); Jabez (1 Chronicles 4:9-10); Jephthah (Judges 11:30-31); David (1 Kings 15:5); Moses (Exodus 3:1-4:18); Hannah (1 Samuel 1:27-28); and many others.

PICK YOUR CHALLENGE: For a more immersive experience pick your challenge below and complete it according to the instructions listed. For the best experience and maximum impact complete all activities, exercises, and challenges.

The Book of Warfare Weapons
Chapter 3
Prayer of Consecration

Your Challenge: To what extent will you consecrate yourself unto God? To what extent can God use you before you tell Him to stop?

For A Great Challenge: Complete activities in Chapter #3 of *The Book of Warfare Weapons–Workbook.*

For A Group Challenge: Complete the Group Challenge of Chapter #3 of *The Book of Warfare Weapons–Workbook.*

For A Great Online Challenge: Complete the online activities and challenges in Chapter #3 of *The Book of Warfare Weapons–Outstanding Warrior Challenge (TBOWW-OWC) online challenge at www.tbowowc.com.*

Prayer of Activation: Father, I thank You, and I love You. I love You, Lord, because You first loved me. Because I love You, I want to offer myself to You as a living sacrifice. Draw me closer to You. Have Your way in my life. I surrender my spirit, soul, body, and all of me unto You. I freely yield and surrender my complete will to You. I offer You my self-will in exchange for Your divine will. Please let Your perfect will manage my life. Keep me from lusts and sinful contaminations of this world. Help me to live each day in righteousness, peace, and joy in the Holy Spirit. Lead me to live a life of humility, gratitude, and true holiness. Give me Your Grace to seek only those things that please You. Help me to live a set-apart life unto You. May You accomplish great things through me for Your Glory. May my life be full of testimonies demonstrating Your amazing Grace and power. I submit myself to You Holy Spirit, and I will listen and obey as You lead me. Thank You for accepting me this day as a consecrated vessel unto You. In the Name of Jesus Christ, I pray. Amen.

Chapter 4
Prayer of Dedication
Primary Purpose: To make oneself available for use
Effective Use: Condemnation
Strength: Very strong

Scriptures:
"I can of mine own self do nothing: as I hear, I judge: and my judgment is just; because I seek not mine own will, but the will of the Father which hath sent me" (John 5:30).

"For I came down from Heaven, not to do mine own will, but the will of Him that sent me" (John 6:38).

"Let this mind be in you, which was also in Christ Jesus" (Philippians 2:5).

"I am crucified with Christ: nevertheless, I live; yet not I, but Christ liveth in me: and the life which I now live in the flesh I live by the faith of the Son of God, who loved me, and gave himself for me" (Galatians 2:20).

The Attack: You want to do more for God, but you never follow through with that idea. You find it hard to concentrate or focus on the things of God, for every time you try to focus, you get tired or distracted. You tell yourself that one day you will be used by God. Several years have passed, and you have little to no spiritual fruits to show for them (i.e., souls you either lead to the Lord, encouraged, or baptized; new souls you brought to church, etc.,).

Weapon of Choice: The Prayer of Dedication.

Defensively: It destroys condemnation, distractions, discouragement, stagnation, defeat, darkness, disappointment, shame, embarrassment, demotion, ridicule, fruitlessness, reproach, setbacks, loneliness, and rejection.

Offensively: This is a great weapon to align yourself to your God-ordained purpose. This weapon increases your ability to hear from God and your availability to be used by God.

The Book of Warfare Weapons
Chapter 4
Prayer of Dedication

Important Notes for this Weapon: This is a prayer a person will pray to make more room in their lives for God. It is giving God what is most important to you or giving God your all because of gratitude. It's like when Hannah did not have a child and was barren. She brought herself to the Lord and dedicated herself. She then promised God that if He blessed her with a son, she would give him back to the Lord. God heard her Prayer of Dedication and blessed her with a son named Samuel. And being true to her promise, she dedicated him back to the Lord. Because of her faithfulness to keeping her word, God also gave her several other children, and Samuel was one of the greatest prophets of the Old Testament. God even vouched for Samuel's greatness by allowing none of Samuel's words to fall to the ground. God prospered Samuel for the condition of his heart, but even more so because his mother was willing to make room in her life for God by dedicating her only son to Him.

How to Use this Weapon: While in prayer, let your heart speak to God and determine how much room you will make in your life for Him. It usually requires that you give up something important and replace that time or attention with more of God. As you pray, be willing to be used by God to do whatever He reveals to you (i.e., witness, visit the sick, be baptized, faithfully support a church or ministry, visit orphans, visit those incarcerated, feed the homeless, defend the defenseless, etc.). Be faithfully committed to fulfilling, by His grace, whatever He reveals to you to do.

Secrets of this Weapon: God will use you to the extent that you make yourself available to Him. When you pray the Prayer of Dedication, the light of God will shine on your soul, destroying all powers of darkness that would shroud your path of righteousness.

Weapon's Source of Power: The mighty weapon of the Prayer of Dedication is energized by the light, love, mercy, and Grace of God.

The Book of Warfare Weapons
Chapter 4
Prayer of Dedication

Faith Heroes Using this Weapon: Abraham (Genesis 22); Josiah (2 Kings 23:3); Jacob (Genesis 28:20-22); Jabez (1 Chronicles 4:9-10); Jephthah (Judges 11:30-31); David (1 Kings 15:5); Moses (Exodus 3:1-4:18); Hannah (1 Samuel 1:27-28); and many others.

PICK YOUR CHALLENGE: For a more immersive experience pick your challenge below and complete it according to the instructions listed. For the best experience and maximum impact complete all activities, exercises, and challenges.

Your Challenge: How often can God depend on you? Can God count on you to fulfill His will, even if it is uncomfortable, or costs you dearly to do it? To what extent will you dedicate yourself to God?

For A Great Challenge: Complete activities in Chapter #4 of *The Book of Warfare Weapons—Workbook*.

For A Group Challenge: Complete the Group Challenge of Chapter #4 of *The Book of Warfare Weapons—Workbook*.

For A Great Online Challenge: Complete the online activities and challenges in Chapter #4 of *The Book of Warfare Weapons—Outstanding Warrior Challenge (TBOWW-OWC) online challenge* at www.tbowowc.com.

Prayer of Activation: Heavenly Father, I thank You that You freely gave Your only Son, Jesus, as the ransom for my sin. Jesus died and rose again that I might have life more abundantly. Thank You, God, for giving me the gift of eternal life. Now that I have eternal life, I want to dedicate myself to doing Your complete will. Let Your Word fill my heart. Let Your love flood my soul. Let Your Holy Spirit fill me with baptism fire. Give me the grace to fulfill Your will, with excellence, in the spiritual field that You have assigned to me. Help me love You, and serve You faithfully by Your Spirit, all the days of my life. I want to hear You say, "Well done, thou good and faithful servant." By Your Grace, I believe that I shall. In the Name of Jesus Christ, I pray. Amen.

The Book of Warfare Weapons
Chapter 5
Prayer of Faith
Primary Purpose: To connect to the power of Heaven
Effective Use: All enemies
Strength: Unlimited

Scripture:
"And the prayer of faith shall save the sick, and the Lord shall raise him up; and if he hath committed sins, they shall be forgiven him" (James 5:15).
 "Therefore I say unto you, What things soever ye desire, when ye pray, believe that you receive them, and ye shall have them" (Mark 11:22-24).

The Attack: You or a loved one is sick, very sick; perhaps you or a loved one is on a death bed. You face a situation where the odds are against you, and your chances for success are slim to none. You are dealing with something that your human effort can't fix or resolve. Powers, authorities, systems, or organizations might have moved against you to witness your defeat. What will you do?

Weapon of Choice: The Prayer of Faith.

Defensively: This weapon is effective against all the forces of darkness, but especially against sicknesses, diseases, disasters, failures, defeat, fear, doubt, unbelief, troubles, bad news, calamity, death sentences, curses, bondage, addictions, demon possessions, yokes, poverty, insanity, and many more.

Offensively: This is a mighty weapon that connects the believer to the unlimited power of God. This weapon pleases God. It gives the believer power in Heaven and on earth to alter the laws of nature as is necessary to promote the extension of each person's God-given purpose.

Important Notes for this Weapon: The Prayer of Faith is so powerful that it is the faith of God manifesting through prayer. It's when a person gets to a certain level of prayer, and the actual faith of God begins to flow through them. Some people have it as a gift, and some have it as an anointing, but it is something we all need to please God. You don't need truckloads of faith. Jesus said if we have faith just the size of a mustard seed (the smallest of seeds), we can say to the mountain (the problem, the illness, the addiction, etc.), "*Be thou removed, be though plucked up and cast into the sea and it shall obey us, and nothing will be impossible to him that believe*" (Mark 11:23). Therefore, the Prayer of Faith is a prayer that brings the miracle-working power of God into your life.

How to Use this Weapon: When you pray, focus on believing everything that the Word of God has to say about a situation, knowing it is the final authority concerning everything in Heaven, on earth, or under the earth. See yourself as if you are standing before God in the throne room court of Heaven. The enemy is trying to resist you on earth, but as long as you cling to the Word of God as your evidence, promise, and answer, then you will always prevail. Now, prove to God through your prayer and continual faith confession that you truly believe His Word. Rely on it to sustain you and to give you victory over the enemy. After praying, rejoice before God with thanksgiving and praise, expecting the answer to manifest in time.

Secrets of this Weapon: It is the faith of God that the Holy Spirit transports and deposits into the heart of the believer as he abides in Christ and feasts upon the Word of God.

Weapon's Source of Power: The life-changing weapon called the Prayer of Faith is energized by the Almighty presence of God. The "spiritual God-substance" that God used to frame the worlds, He now shares with His children. The power in it derives from the very presence of Almighty God and travels by means of the Word.

Faith Heroes Using this Weapon: All the faith heroes of Hebrews Chapter 11, and every person who will ever please God. For without faith, it is impossible to please God (Hebrews 11:6).

The Book of Warfare Weapons
Chapter 5
Prayer of Faith

PICK YOUR CHALLENGE: For a more immersive experience pick your challenge below and complete it according to the instructions listed.
For the best experience and maximum impact complete all the activities, exercises, and challenges.

Your Challenge: How do you recognize the Prayer of Faith? Pray with confidence while releasing yourself from all restrictions of fear, doubt, and unbelief. Believe that what you have prayed for, by faith you currently possess.

For A Great Challenge: Complete activities in Chapter #5 of *The Book of Warfare Weapons–Workbook.*

For A Group Challenge: Complete the Group Challenge of Chapter #5 of *The Book of Warfare Weapons–Workbook.*

For A Great Online Challenge: Complete the online activities and challenges in Chapter #5 of *The Book of Warfare Weapons–Outstanding Warrior Challenge (TBOWW-OWC) online challenge* at _www.tbowowc.com._

Prayer of Activation: Father, thank You for giving me the God-substance called faith by which I can access Your miracle-working power. You said that nothing would be impossible for us if we have faith the size of a mustard seed. I have mustard seed-sized faith in that I believe Jesus Christ to be my Lord and Savior. Now, I release my mustard seed-sized faith in this, my prayer to You (Pray your prayer request). By faith, I believe that You hear my prayer, and I receive what I have asked of You. Thank You, Heavenly Father, for answering my prayer. In the Name of Jesus Christ, I pray. Amen.

Please note: Everyone does not have the same measure of faith (Romans 12:6). Yet, even the person with mustard seed-sized faith can move trees and mountains. Also, your faith can increase by hearing the Word of God daily.

The Book of Warfare Weapons
Chapter 6
Prayer of Forgiveness
Primary Purpose: To reconcile, set free, and cover offenses
Effective Use: Unforgiveness and bitterness
Strength: Extremely strong

Scriptures:
"Then said Jesus *Father, forgive them; for they know not what they do*"
(Luke 23:34).
"And they stoned Stephen…And he kneeled, and cried with a loud voice,
"Lord, lay not this sin to their charge." And when he had said this, he fell
asleep" (Acts 7:59-60).

The Attack: Someone has wronged you or offended you. You can't get the
offense out of your mind. The very sight or thought of the person makes
you disgusted or angry; therefore, you prefer to avoid the person at all costs.
Nothing they can say or do will make things right with you.

Weapon of Choice: Prayer of Forgiveness.

Defensively: This weapon is highly effective in keeping the heart from
becoming contaminated with evil, bitterness, and unforgiveness. It is also
effective against reproaches, ridicule, hatred, bigotry, transgressions,
trespasses, hurts, scars, betrayals, deception, broken hearts, rage, violence,
impatience, revenge, regrets, and hard-heartedness.

Offensively: This weapon is especially effective for mending broken
relationships and for destroying all offenses. This weapon is excellent for
bringing peace to environments where there is strife.

How to Use this Weapon: The Bible reveals, "we have all sinned and have
come short of the Glory of God." All of us need God's forgiveness. The
Bible says if we do not forgive others for their trespasses, neither will God
forgive us our trespasses (Mark 11:26). We must always forgive people.
Forgiveness doesn't mean that the other person deserves forgiveness. We
forgive them, not because they deserve it, but because it is the heavenly,
mandatory requirement for us to receive forgiveness from God.

The Book of Warfare Weapons
Chapter 6
Prayer of Forgiveness

We must give forgiveness to others as a requirement for us to receive forgiveness from God. If God can forgive us for our sins and the messes we've made, then we can truly forgive others for the sins and offenses they have committed against us. The perfect example of forgiveness is Jesus Christ hanging on the cross. Bleeding and in excruciating pain, Jesus looked at his tormentors, haters, and mockers, and then He prayed for them. He looked up to Heaven and said, "Father, forgive them, for they know not what they do" (Luke 23:34). Jesus showed us the most remarkable example of one praying the Prayer of Forgiveness.

Secrets of this Weapon: It is God's antidote against all offenses.

Weapon's Source of Power: The incredible weapon called the Prayer of Forgiveness is energized by God's love. God forgives us of all our trespasses, offenses, and sins. The same love that we receive commands us and empowers us to forgive others. If we refuse, then it is evident that we have not received His love, and we are still living in our sins.

Faith Heroes Using this Weapon: *Our perfect example is Jesus Christ (Luke 23:34); Stephen (Acts 7:60); Moses (Exodus 32:31-32); Job (Job 42:8-10); Paul (2 Corinthians 2:10); and many others used it as well.

PICK YOUR CHALLENGE: For a more immersive experience pick your challenge below and complete it according to the instructions listed.
For the best experience and maximum impact complete all activities, exercises, and challenges.

Your Challenge: Who are the people who have offended, betrayed, or hurt you? Are you willing to forgive them so that you can receive forgiveness? What is the evidence of your forgiveness?

17

The Book of Warfare Weapons
Chapter 6
Prayer of Forgiveness

For A Great Challenge: Complete activities in Chapter #6 of *The Book of Warfare Weapons–Workbook.*

For A Group Challenge: Complete the Group Challenge of Chapter #6 of *The Book of Warfare Weapons–Workbook.*

For A Great Online Challenge: Complete the online activities and challenges in Chapter #6 of *The Book of Warfare Weapons–Outstanding Warrior Challenge (TBOWW-OWC) online challenge at* www.tbowowc.com.

Prayer of Activation: Heavenly Father, I thank You that it was on the cross that Jesus shed His precious Blood to forgive me of all my sins. Jesus bore all my offenses and transgressions so that I could go free. As a condition of receiving Your forgiveness, I am obligated and commanded to forgive others. By the power of Your Grace and Holy Spirit, I yield myself to freely and openly forgive _____ for what (he, she, they) did to me. I do not forgive because they deserve it (for I do not deserve forgiveness either). I forgive so that both of us may be healed and made better when Your divine love flows through our hearts. Heal me now, Heavenly Father, from all hurt associated with the offenses and transgressions I experienced. Let Your Holy Spirit wash my memory, heart, and emotions so that I will not remember the hurts anymore. Help mature the other person to do better and help me not be easily offended in the future. By Your Grace, I forgive _____. I pray, Heavenly Father, that You will forgive _____ also. Thank You for giving me grace, love, and the strength to forgive _____, as You have forgiven me. In the Name of Jesus Christ, I pray. Amen.

The Book of Warfare Weapons
Chapter 7
Prayer of Repentance
Primary Purpose: To bring about salvation and restoration
Effective Use: Sins, transgressions, and offenses
Strength: Extremely strong

Scriptures:

"If my people, which are called by my name, shall humble themselves, and pray, and seek my face, and turn from their wicked ways; then will I hear from heaven, and will forgive their sin, and will heal their land" (2 Chronicles 7:14).

"He that covereth his sins shall not prosper: but whoso confesseth and forsaketh them shall have mercy" (Proverbs 28:13).

The Attack: You have made a mistake or offended another person. You hurt people, and now you are genuinely sorry for doing so. You want to make things right, but you're not sure if the other person will give you a chance to do so. You wish you could reconnect with family, friends, or loved ones from whom you are now estranged because of your past offense.

Weapon of Choice: The Prayer of Repentance.

Defensively: This is a mighty weapon to destroy offenses, transgressions, and sin. It also effectively destroys hatred, self-righteousness, pride, prejudices, bigotry, sexism, disobedience, and rebellion.

Offensively: This weapon is so powerful that it allows one to receive countless blessings from God and even to receive God's gift of eternal life through Jesus Christ. This weapon also helps you to walk in peace with God and mankind.

How to Use this Weapon: The Prayer of Repentance is when a person prays to ask forgiveness for their sins before God. You should also pray this prayer if you have offended another person. Before you repent to the person, first ask God to forgive you, then go and apologize to the person you offended. Ask the person you have offended to forgive you. God loves this type of prayer because it involves a person having a broken

19

heart before Him. It's not just saying "I am sorry," nor is it merely feeling bad because you got caught. You must be genuinely sorrowful for the pain you have caused another person. True from the heart produces power, enabling one to experience a complete turnaround in his or her life.

Secrets of this Weapon: When this weapon is active, it strips the Accuser of any legal reason to accuse you.

Weapon's Source of Power: This unique weapon called the Prayer of Repentance is energized by the love, humility, righteousness, goodness, and mercy of God.

Faith Heroes Using this Weapon: David (Psalm 51:1-17); Hezekiah (Isaiah 38:1-5); Zacchaeus (Luke 19: 5-10); the thief on the cross (Luke 23:40-42); the prodigal son (Luke 15:18-24); and many others.

PICK YOUR CHALLENGE: For a more immersive experience pick your challenge below and complete it according to the instructions listed. For the best experience and maximum impact complete all activities, exercises, and challenges.

Your Challenge: Confess your faults to God.

For A Great Challenge: Complete activities in Chapter #7 of *The Book of Warfare Weapons–Workbook.*

For A Group Challenge: Complete the Group Challenge of Chapter #7 of *The Book of Warfare Weapons–Workbook.*

For A Great Online Challenge: Complete the online activities and challenges in Chapter #7 of *The Book of Warfare Weapons–Outstanding Warrior Challenge (TBOWW-OWC) online challenge* at *www.tbowowc.com.*

The Book of Warfare Weapons
Chapter 7
Prayer of Repentance

Prayer of Activation: Father, I thank You. It is through Jesus' shed Blood that I am forgiven. For without the shedding of Blood, there would be no remission of sin. Your Word says that if we confess our sins, You are faithful and just to forgive us of all sins and to cleanse us from all unrighteousness. I repent of the sins and wrong I committed against_____. I confess that it is wrong, and I need Your forgiveness. I ask You to please forgive me. Also, because I have sinned against_____, please let him/her accept my repentance and also forgive me. Help me to make amends to anyone I have wronged when it is in my power to do so (which is a true sign of repentance and righteousness). Now, Father, by the power of Your Holy Spirit, help me also to forgive myself. I believe by faith that I am forgiven and that You will help _____ to forgive me. Thank You for the grace of repentance. I receive it now. I thank You for hearing me and answering my prayer through the Holy Spirit. In the Name of Jesus Christ, I pray. Amen.

Chapter 8
Praise

Primary Purpose: To access glory and deliverance
Effective Use: Deliverance from many
Strength: Very strong

Scriptures:

"Out of the mouth of babes and sucklings hast thou ordained strength because of thine enemies, that thou mightiest still the enemy and the avenger" (Psalm 8:2).

"And the shepherds returned, glorifying and praising God for all the things that they had heard and seen, as it was told unto them" (Luke 2:20).

"And immediately he received his sight, and followed him, glorifying God: and all the people, when they saw it, gave praise unto God" (Luke 18:43).

The Attack: You find yourself plagued with worries, anxiety, phobias, sadness, worthlessness, hopelessness, or depression. Fear terrorizes your life continually. You want to be happy and have joy, but it is a struggle. You want to be able to dwell in the presence of the Lord continually, despite the ups and downs of your situation or life surroundings.

Weapon of Choice: Praise.

Defensively: It is especially effective against worries, anxiety, phobias, hopelessness, oppression, numbness, bondages, captivity, sabotages, complaining, heaviness, depression, terror, nightmares, thoughts of death, and doom, worthlessness, and sadness.

Offensively: Praise is a powerful weapon that can bring victory in any situation. It is excellent for all types of deliverance and breakthroughs. However, it is especially effective for accelerating the delivery of prayer requests and blessings.

How to Use this Weapon: Praise is a powerful weapon, for it ushers the glory of God into an environment. It destroys the plots and plans of the enemy. If a person is in any trouble, God begins to set them free when they start to Praise.

The Book of Warfare Weapons
Chapter 8
Prayer of Praise

For example, when Israel was going out to battle and began to sing praises, God sent ambushments against their enemies. Paul and Silas were in the Roman jail and began singing and praising, and God shook the prison, and all the shackles fell off. So, this is great for individuals experiencing situations of destruction or captivity. When they begin to sing praises or pray praises unto God, miraculous things will occur.

Secrets of this Weapon: It is intentionally focusing on God. It is coming to the realization that God is completely good at all times and that He has done great things. It also sees God as being bigger than your problems or situation and gives Him glory for it.

Weapon's Source of Power: The mighty weapon called Praise is energized by the goodness of God and the finished work of Jesus Christ. Praise is a holy sacrifice offered to God. When we offer Praise, God is glorified and pleased. God then accepts our holy sacrifice by inhabiting our Praise. His presence in our Praise sends forth deliverance to every area of our lives.

Faith Heroes Using this Weapon: King Jehoshaphat's miraculous victory (2 Chronicles 20:22); David (1 Samuel 16:23); all Israel (Ezra 3:11); Paul and Silas (Acts 16:25-26); and many more.

PICK YOUR CHALLENGE: For a more immersive experience pick your challenge below and complete it according to the instructions listed. For the best experience and maximum impact complete all activities, exercises, and challenges.

Your Challenge: Practice offering God a certain number of praises each day, then slowly increase it over time.

The Book of Warfare Weapons
Chapter 8
Prayer of Praise

For A Great Challenge: Complete activities in Chapter #8 of *The Book of Warfare Weapons–Workbook.*

For A Group Challenge: Complete the Group Challenge of Chapter #8 of *The Book of Warfare Weapons–Workbook*
.

For A Great Online Challenge: Complete the online activities and challenges in Chapter #8 of *The Book of Warfare Weapons–Outstanding Warrior Challenge (TBOWW-OWC) at www.tbowowc.com.*

Prayer of Activation: Father, I bless Your name. Thank You for putting a new song in my heart. I Praise You for Your mighty acts, for Your excellent greatness, and for who You are to me. It is my reasonable service to offer praises to You. You are truly worthy of all Praise, honor, and glory. I offer You this prayer of Praise to let You know that I truly love and appreciate You. I hope that it helps to make Your day. I love You, God. (Think of about 25 things for which you are thankful. Tell God, then offer Praise for each one of them). Hallelujah! God, I Praise You for_____. Thank You, God! (Repeat with another Praise, and continue until you finish the list), thank You for hearing my prayer through the Holy Spirit. In the Name of Jesus Christ, I pray. Amen.

The Book of Warfare Weapons
Chapter 9
Prayer of Petition

Primary Purpose: To fulfill the desires of your heart
Effective Use: Many enemies
Strength: Strong

Scriptures: "And if we know that he hears us, whatsoever we ask, we know that we have the petitions that we desired of him" (1 John 5:15).
"Ask, and it shall be given you; seek, and you shall find; knock, and it shall be opened unto you" (Matthew 7:7).

The Attack: You have a need in your life or want to receive something from God.

Weapon of Choice: Prayer of Petition.

Defensively: This is a potent weapon that is effective against lack, poverty, emptiness, fruitlessness, insufficiency, dryness, disappointments, injustice, and missed opportunities.

Offensively: The Prayer of Petition is an excellent weapon for receiving the desires of your heart. It is also great for accessing all the treasures of Heaven.

How to Use this Weapon: The Prayer of Petition is the most common type of prayer that everybody knows and that everybody prays. It's the one prayer that we've learned since we were kids. In this prayer, you are simply asking God for things. It's okay to ask God for things, for Jesus told us to do so. The Bible says to cast all your cares on Him because He cares for you (1 Peter 5:7). It also says that God will give you the desires of your heart if you delight yourself in Him (Psalm 37:4). When you use the Prayer of Petition, you must remember to ask for things that please God, not just for things that please your flesh.

Secrets of this Weapon: The Prayer of Petition is a spiritual transaction, whereas you execute a withdrawal from God's riches in Heaven to materialize on Earth.

Weapon's Source of Power: This powerful weapon called the Prayer of Petition is energized by God's love, goodness, and covenant promises.

25

The Book of Warfare Weapons
Chapter 9
Prayer of Petition

Faith Heroes Using this Weapon: The majority of all believers use this Prayer of Petition weapon, for it is one of the first prayers that we learned to pray as children. It is simply asking God to give us the desires of our hearts according to His Word (Matthew 7:7-8). Please note: You can only receive the measure that you are able to believe.

PICK YOUR CHALLENGE: For a more immersive experience pick your challenge below and complete it according to the instructions listed.
For the best experience and maximum impact complete all activities, exercises, and challenges.

Your Challenge: Start a prayer journal asking God to grant you the petitions or desires of your heart (Psalm 37:4).

For A Great Challenge: Complete activities in Chapter #9 of *The Book of Warfare Weapons–Workbook*.

For A Group Challenge: Complete the Group Challenge of Chapter #9 of *The Book of Warfare Weapons–Workbook*.

For A Great Online Challenge: Complete the online activities and challenges in Chapter #9 of *The Book of Warfare Weapons–Outstanding Warrior Challenge (TBOWW-OWC) online challenge* at *www.tbowowc.com*.

Prayer of Activation: Father, I thank You that it's because of Jesus Christ, I can come boldly to the throne of Grace. Thank You that I can obtain mercy to help me in this time of need. Thank You also for allowing me to cast all my cares upon You, for You care for me. Father, You told me that I have not because I ask not. Your Word says to ask, and I shall receive. I ask You now for (tell Him your requests) _____. I believe now that I have that which I ask of You, through the Holy Spirit. I thank You for it, Father. In the Name of Jesus Christ, I pray. Amen

The Book of Warfare Weapons
Chapter 10
Prayer of Intercession
Primary Purpose: To send help to others
Effective Use: Against destruction and captivity
Strength: Very strong

Scriptures:

"I exhort therefore, that, first of all, supplications, prayers, intercessions, and giving of thanks, be made for all men" (1 Timothy 2:1).

"And the men turned their faces from thence, and went toward Sodom: but Abraham stood yet before the Lord. And Abraham drew near, and said, "Wilt thou also destroy the righteous with the wicked? Peradventure there be fifty righteous within the city: wilt thou also destroy and not spare the place for the fifty righteous that are therein? That be far from thee to do after this manner, to slay the righteous with the wicked: and that the righteous should be as the wicked, that be far from thee: shall not the Judge of all the earth do right?" And the Lord said, "If I find in Sodom fifty righteous within the city, then I will spare all the place for their sakes." And Abraham answered and said, "Behold now, I have taken upon me to speak unto the Lord, which am but dust and ashes: Peradventure there shall lack five of the fifty righteous: wilt thou destroy all the city for lack of five?" And he said, "If I find there forty and five, I will not destroy it." And he spake unto him yet again, and said, "Peradventure there shall be forty found there." And he said, "I will not do it for forty's sake." And he said unto him, "Oh let not the Lord be angry, and I will speak: Peradventure there shall thirty be found there." And he said, "I will not do it if I find thirty there." And he said, "Behold now, I have taken upon me to speak unto the Lord: Peradventure there shall be twenty found there," And he said, "I will not destroy it for twenty's sake." And he said, "Oh let not the Lord be angry, and I will speak yet but this once: Peradventure ten shall be found there." And he said, "I will not destroy it for ten's sake." And the Lord went his way, as soon as he had left communing with Abraham; and Abraham returned unto his place" (Genesis 18:22-33).

The Book of Warfare Weapons
Chapter 10
Prayer of Intercession

The Attack: You see a person going through troubles or who is about to be under spiritual attack. You know someone who has experienced or is about to experience judgment, punishment, hard times, or they are unsaved.

Weapon of Choice: The Prayer of Intercession.

Defensively: This is a mighty weapon to deliver from judgments, disaster, and captivity. It is also effective against divorce, foreclosure, bankruptcy, repossession, disease, injustice, injury, addictions, bondage, incarceration, and rebellion.

Offensively: This weapon can cause mercy, grace, rescue, deliverance, healing, and favor to fall on anyone at any time.

How to Use this Weapon: What is intercession? Intercession is you using your personal access to God's asking Him to extend a measure of His unlimited goodness to another person. The Bible lets us know that whatever we ask in prayer, believing, we shall receive. And as children of the Most High God, certain benefits are afforded to us who are saved. So, you use your benefits to intercede on behalf of another person so that he or she will be blessed, saved, healed, delivered, or set free. The perfect example of this is Abraham. He was praying and interceding to God on behalf of his nephew, Lot, not to be destroyed with Sodom. God heard and answered his prayer.

Secrets of this Weapon: God's love and compassion for others manifested through prayer. It is God's creative way of allowing people to receive additional blessings that they may not be entitled to receive or may not know belong to them.

Weapon's Source of Power: This mighty weapon called the Prayer of Intercession is energized by the exalted position of Jesus Christ, as He intercedes for us in Heaven (Romans 8:34). The love, compassion, mercy, and kindness of God increase in the believer's heart the more he or she uses this weapon.

The Book of Warfare Weapons
Chapter 10
Prayer of Intercession

Faith Heroes Using this Weapon: Abraham for Lot (Genesis 18:17-33); Jesus (Romans 8:34); Holy Spirit (Romans 8:26); and Peter (Acts 12:5).

PICK YOUR CHALLENGE: For a more immersive experience pick your challenge below and complete it according to the instructions listed. For the best experience and maximum impact complete all activities, exercises, and challenges.

Your Challenge: Make a list of people who you can intercede for today/this week. Pray for those people each day for seven days.

For A Great Challenge: Complete activities in Chapter #10 of *The Book of Warfare Weapons–Workbook*.

For A Group Challenge: Complete the Group Challenge of Chapter #10 of *The Book of Warfare Weapons–Workbook*.

For A Great Online Challenge: Complete the online activities and challenges in Chapter #10 of *The Book of Warfare Weapons–Outstanding Warrior Challenge (TBOWW-OWC) online challenge at* _www.tbowowc.com_.

Prayer of Activation: Father, I thank You that Jesus is at Your right hand, interceding for me in Heaven. I thank You that the Holy Spirit is interceding for me on earth. Thank You for also giving me the secret of intercession, wherein I can intercede for others. I intercede for_____(*pray for each person on your intercession list, name by name and one by one*). I intercede for this person, and I ask You to _____ him or her. Fix things in their lives. Help them to come to know You as Lord and Savior. May their names be written in Your Lamb's Book of Life. Please chase away the evil one from them. Help them to walk in love, righteousness, and true holiness. May they come to fulfill Your purpose for their lives. I thank You, Father, for hearing and answering my prayer through the Holy Spirit. In the Name of Jesus Christ, I pray. Amen.

The Book of Warfare Weapons
Chapter 11
Prayer of Supplication
Primary Purpose: To access miracles
Effective Use: Impossible situations
Strength: Unlimited

Scriptures:
"Praying always with all prayer and supplication in the Spirit, and watching thereunto with all perseverance and supplication for all saints" (Ephesians 6:18). "And I set my face unto the Lord God, to seek by prayer and supplications, with fasting, and sackcloth, and ashes" (Daniel 9:3).

The Attack: You need a miracle from God. You are under a severe spiritual attack, your prayer request has been held up for a long time, or you sense it is time for your breakthrough from God, or you want to defend your breakthrough from being aborted.

Weapon of Choice: The Prayer of Supplication.

Defensively: This weapon can give you victory over all the powers of darkness and wickedness. It is especially effective when dealing with death sentences, death decrees, terminal situations, mental illnesses, and times when there appears no way out, or all hope seems lost.

Offensively: This is a life-altering weapon of unlimited power that can produce miracles, signs, and wonders of unbelievable proportions.

How to Use this Weapon: Supplication is that strong crying. It's like crying out from the soul, pleading with God for an answer. It's not just giving a petition, but it's a persistent, absolute, yearning heart, crying continually to God until He gives a breakthrough. It's like praying for a loved one who is on their death bed in the hospital. You don't just say it one time: "God, please heal my loved one." If that person is close to you, then you yearn before God. Your heart cries out from a place deep within your soul. It is a refusal to give up until you receive your answer. The Bible describes Jesus praying this way. He prayed for an hour, three times on the night that He was betrayed, saying, "*God, if it is possible, let this cup pass,*" and His sweat fell to the ground as if it were drops of blood (Luke 22:44). That was supplication at its most potent and most intense level. He was persistent before God to receive a breakthrough. And, He got His victory at the end of the third Prayer of Supplication.

Secrets of this Weapon: It is like grabbing the horns of the spiritual altar and refusing to let go. Jacob wrestled with the angel and refused to go until the angel blessed him (Genesis 32:26). Jacob wrestling with the angel in the Old Testament was a "shadow-and-type" of the benefits that one can receive through supplication.

Weapon's Source of Power: This life-changing weapon called the Prayer of Supplication is energized by the suffering passion of Jesus Christ. Jesus suffered beyond measure and freely made His soul an offering for sin so that you and I can be free. Jesus can have compassion on us because He too, experienced our suffering. He willingly bore all our sufferings upon Himself on the cross to give us victory over them.

Faith Heroes Using this Weapon: Jesus, with strong crying and tears (Hebrews 5:7-8); Jacob (Hosea 12:4); Job (Job 1:5); Hannah (1 Samuel 1:6-10); David (2 Samuel 2:12-23); Cornelius (Acts 10:4); and many others.

PICK YOUR CHALLENGE: For a more immersive experience pick your challenge below and complete it according to the instructions listed.
For the best experience and maximum impact complete all activities, exercises, and challenges.

Your Challenge: In what ways can you add supplication to your prayer? Pray the prayer of supplication this week and track all results in your prayer journal.

For A Great Challenge: Complete activities in Chapter #11 of *The Book of Warfare Weapons–Workbook.*

The Book of Warfare Weapons
Chapter 11
Prayer of Supplication

For A Group Challenge: Complete the Group Challenge of Chapter #11 of *The Book of Warfare Weapons–Workbook.*

For A Great Online Challenge: Complete the online activities and challenges in Chapter #11 of *The Book of Warfare Weapons–Outstanding Warrior Challenge (TBOWW-OWC) online challenge at* <u>www.tbowowc.com.</u>

Prayer of Activation: Father, I thank You that You always hear my prayers. I thank You that Jesus Christ has given me victory that overcomes the whole world. I thank You that, through the victory of Your life, You conquered the power of death. I know that nothing is impossible for You. You possess both creative power and resurrection power that can change my situation. You specialize in working wonders. Now, because my opposition is strong, I supplicate before You with earnest desire. I know You are stronger and greater than all opposition. I have a desire (or a need) that is so great only You can fulfill it. I ask You, Father, to please (now make your requests) _____.

(*Stay there, before God, and share with Him every promise of His Word you can find that assures you of the answer. This type of prayer is not a fast or quick prayer, but a continual embracing and petitioning for an answer and a mighty move of God*). I thank you, Father, that I have that I ask of you through the Holy Spirit. In the Name of Jesus Christ, I pray. Amen.

The Book of Warfare Weapons
Chapter 12
Prayer of Thanksgiving
Primary Purpose: To access favor
Effective Use: Murmuring and complaining
Strength: Very strong

Scriptures: "Be careful for nothing; but in every thing by prayer and supplication with thanksgiving let your requests be made known unto God" (Philippians 4:6). "Continue in prayer, and watch in the same with thanksgiving" (Colossians 4:2).

The Attack: You notice that you have been murmuring, grumbling, and complaining quite often lately. You notice that your conversations are full of negative, shocking, or troubling news. You are sad, lacking joy, oppressed, agitated, irritated, sensitive, pessimistic, or easily angered.

Weapon of Choice: The Prayer of Thanksgiving.

Defensively: This dynamic weapon effectively destroys all negativity, bondage, and oppression from the enemy. It is also effective against sadness, lack of joy, oppression, suppression, depression, agitation, irritability, sensitivity, pessimism, anger, rage, complaining, gossip, discord, lies, cursing, profanity, filthy language, hatred, bigotry, violence, and lack of control.

Offensively: This weapon is effective in returning glory and honor to God. It destroys all hindrances attempting to block or delay your blessings. It makes you an eligible receiver of the blessings of God.

How to Use this Weapon: We are commanded to give thanks (1 Thessalonians 5:18). We all know how to offer thanksgiving, but there is something more God wants from His people. God desires His people to offer thanks continually, knowing that our whole life is complete in Jesus Christ. The more a person offers thanksgiving from a grateful heart, the more they send up praises to God, then more blessings will come down. So, God desires that everything we offer to Him, we offer it with a grateful heart of thanksgiving.

The Book of Warfare Weapons
Chapter 12
Prayer of Thanksgiving

Secrets of this Weapon: In the spirit realm, all prayers receive answers the moment they are prayed in faith, but the delivery of those answered prayers can be held up according to one's attitude. A person remains an ineligible receiver of the manifestation of their answered prayers until they choose to offer thanksgiving. Thanksgiving releases the answer to all prayer requests and all Godly things our hearts desire. It releases blessings, grace, and the favor of God.

Weapon's Source of Power: This mighty weapon called the Prayer of Thanksgiving is energized by the goodness of God. We tap into the goodness of God, the joy of God, the favor of God, and the love of God each time we use this weapon.

Faith Heroes Using this Weapon: David, Asaph, Zerubbabel, Nehemiah (Nehemiah 12:46-47); One leper from the ten (Luke 17:11-19); Woman with the alabaster box (Luke 7:37-50); King Solomon and Israel (2 Chronicles 5:13-14); and many more.

PICK YOUR CHALLENGE: For a more immersive experience pick your challenge below and complete it according to the instructions listed. For the best experience and maximum impact complete all activities, exercises, and challenges.

Your Challenge: Practice giving thanks in all situations and continually throughout each day.

For A Great Challenge: Complete activities in Chapter #12 of *The Book of Warfare Weapons–Workbook.*

For A Group Challenge: Complete the Group Challenge of Chapter #12 of *The Book of Warfare Weapons–Workbook.*

The Book of Warfare Weapons
Chapter 12
Prayer of Thanksgiving

For A Great Online Challenge: Complete the online activities and challenges in Chapter #12 of *The Book of Warfare Weapons–Outstanding Warrior Challenge (TBOWW-OWC) online challenge at* <u>www.tbowowc.com</u>.

Prayer of Activation: Father, I want to thank You for life, health, strength, mobility, sensibility, and the blood running warm in my veins. Thank You for Your love, mercy, goodness, gentleness, meekness, joy, peace, longsuffering, and faith. Thank You for living a righteous life, suffering for my transgressions, dying for my redemption, being buried for my atonement, rising for my justification, and ascending for my sanctification. Thank You that You will return for my glorification. Thank You for the cross, Your shed Blood, the Word of God, and the Holy Spirit Baptism. Thank You for mercy, favor, compassion, and grace. Thank You, God, for

_____ (*list everything else that you can think of*). I thank You, Father, for giving me this fantastic opportunity to offer thanks through the Holy Spirit. I love You, and I appreciate You. In the Name of Jesus Christ, I pray. Amen.

The Book of Warfare Weapons
Chapter 13
Prayer of Warfare
Primary Purpose: To claim victory over spiritual attacks
Effective Use: All enemies
Strength: Unlimited

Scriptures:

"(For the weapons of our warfare are not carnal, but mighty through God to the pulling down of strong holds;) Casting down imaginations, and every high thing that exalteth itself against the knowledge of God, and bringing into captivity every thought to the obedience of Christ" (2 Corinthians 10:4-5).

"This charge I commit unto thee, son Timothy, according to the prophecies which went before on thee, that thou by them mightest war a good warfare" (1 Timothy 1:18).

The Attack: You are under a harassing spiritual attack, or have recently come out of one, or your plans have all ended in disaster, or you are expecting a breakthrough, but the answer is held up.

Weapon of Choice: The Prayer of Warfare.

Defensively: This weapon is effective at destroying all plans, strategies, and schemes of the enemy that are active against you.

Offensively: This is a powerful weapon for obtaining continual victory in Christ Jesus in all areas of your life. This weapon helps to clear your pathway and to make your way easy. It ushers in immediate spiritual victories in specific areas of your life.

How to Use this Weapon: The Prayer of Warfare gives you victory over spiritual attacks. The Holy Spirit wants to lead you to exercise victory, power, and authority over evil opposition and attacks through prayer. A perfect example of this is when the whole Syrian army came to arrest the prophet, Elisha. When they came to his house, he did not fear because he flowed in the strength and power of God.

The Book of Warfare Weapons
Chapter 13
Prayer of Warfare

His servant Gehazi, on the other hand, was gripped by fear. So, the prophet Elisha prayed that God would open the eyes of his servant Gehazi so that Gehazi could also see what the mighty prophet was seeing in the spirit realm. And when God opened the eyes of Gehazi, he could see the armies of God and fiery chariots all around the mountaintops and hills, ready to come down and do battle to defend the man of God. So, Elisha prayed again that God would blind the attacking army. God answered and blinded the whole Syrian army according to the prayer of Elisha. Thus, the prophet was able to capture the entire army single-handedly. Therefore, we too are ordained to have victory over all opposition and spiritual attacks by praying warfare prayers through the power of the Holy Spirit.

Secrets of this Weapon: In the spirit realm, it is like you are receiving top-secret intel from the Holy Spirit that directs your prayer in a way that destroys and defeats all approaching, planned, or reserved attacks from the enemy.

Weapon's Source of Power: This life-changing weapon called the Prayer of Warfare is energized by the power of the Holy Spirit. When a saint is baptized in the Holy Spirit, this weapon can be exercised continually. It can be activated in the native tongue or spiritual tongues. However, it is more powerful when activated by speaking in tongues. The enemy knows this and fights relentlessly to keep saints from receiving spiritual tongues from God.

Faith Heroes Using this Weapon: Elisha and the Syrian army (2 Kings 6:8-20); Moses (Exodus 17:11); Joshua (Joshua 10:11-14); David (2 Samuel 5:22-25); King Hezekiah (2 Kings 19:15-19, *35). (*Note: one angel slew 185,000 armed enemies in one night).

PICK YOUR CHALLENGE: For a more immersive experience pick your challenge below and complete it according to the instructions listed.
For the best experience and maximum impact complete all activities, exercises, and challenges.

The Book of Warfare Weapons
Chapter 13
Prayer of Warfare

Your Challenge: Add warfare praying to your arsenal of spiritual weaponry. (Go to www.thebookofwarfare.com and listen to the audio teaching, called *Prepared for Battle*, for examples of how to pray warfare prayers).

For A Great Challenge: Complete activities in Chapter #13 of *The Book of Warfare Weapons–Workbook.*

For A Group Challenge: Complete the Group Challenge of Chapter #13 of *The Book of Warfare Weapons–Workbook.*

For A Great Online Challenge: Complete the online activities and challenges in Chapter #13 of *The Book of Warfare Weapons–Outstanding Warrior Challenge (TBOWW-OWC) online challenge at* www.tbowowc.com.

Prayer of Activation: Father, I thank You that Jesus Christ has defeated all the enemies of mankind by His death, burial, resurrection, and ascension into Heaven. I decree that Jesus Christ defeated Satan, sin, death, Hell, the grave, and all the armies of darkness when He arose on "Resurrection Morning." Now, by faith, I access the power of the resurrection to destroy the powers of darkness that are now opposing me. I declare that Jesus is in me, and all who would fight me are not fighting me, but the living Christ who lives in me. I can't be defeated when I turn the battle over to the Lord, for the battle is not mine, but the Lord's. I thank you, God, that Your Blood covers me because I am your child. Now, I pray *(pray your warfare prayer)* _____ by the leading of the Holy Spirit. Thank You, Heavenly Father, for giving me victory. In the Name of Jesus Christ, I pray. Amen.

The Book of Warfare Weapons
Chapter 14
Prayer of Worship
Primary Purpose: To increase intimacy with God
Effective Use: All enemies
Strength: Unlimited

Scriptures:

"And at midnight Paul and Silas prayed, and sang praises unto God: and the prisoners heard them. And suddenly there was a great earthquake, so that the foundations of the prison were shaken: and immediately all the doors were opened, and every one's bands were loosed" (Acts 16:25-26).

"O come, let us worship and bow down: let us kneel before the Lord our maker. For he is our God; and we are the people of his pasture, and the sheep of his hand" (Psalm 95:6-7a).

The Attack: You find it hard to sing songs to Jesus. You find it difficult or boring to honor or reverence God in a personal way. It has been a long time since you bowed down or knelt before God to worship Him. Fellowshipping with God seems like a waste of time, as you could be doing something more productive.

Weapon of Choice: Prayer of Worship.

Defensively: This weapon is effective against stagnation, emptiness, weakness, oppression, error, irreverence, sensuality, pride, self-righteousness, fleshly desires, distractions, self-will, meanness, fornication, pornography, and idolatry.

Offensively: This weapon is effective in increasing your fellowship with God. During worship, you are being transformed into the image of Jesus Christ.

How to Use this Weapon: When a person prays worship prayers, they are in the process of adoring and honoring God in prayer. They must worship in the Spirit and in truth, according to John 4:24.

Secrets of this Weapon: It is like building a platform for a major concert, expecting a headliner to take the stage. Adoring God with the Prayer of Worship sets the stage for His Presence to come on the scene.

The Book of Warfare Weapons
Chapter 14
Prayer of Worship

Weapon's Source of Power: This life-changing weapon called the Prayer of Worship is energized by God's love flowing in the heart of the believer. As God's love fills the believer's heart, it then begins to overflow into filling the spirit, soul, and body. The spirit, soul, and body can respond individually or collectively to God's love. When all three are in unison, then worship is in Spirit and in truth. It is how God desires that we worship Him—with all our hearts, minds, souls, strength, and bodies (Luke 20:27).

Faith Heroes Using this Weapon: All the heroes of faith worshipped God. All saints of God are commanded to worship God in Spirit and in truth (John 4:24).

PICK YOUR CHALLENGE: For a more immersive experience pick your challenge below and complete it according to the instructions listed.
For the best experience and maximum impact complete all activities, exercises, and challenges.

Your Challenge: Worship God without music.

For A Great Challenge: Complete activities in Chapter #14 of *The Book of Warfare Weapons–Workbook.*

For A Group Challenge: Complete the Group Challenge of Chapter #14 of *The Book of Warfare Weapons–Workbook.*

For A Great Online Challenge: Complete the online activities and challenges in Chapter #14 of *The Book of Warfare Weapons–Outstanding Warrior Challenge (TBOWW-OWC) online challenge at* www.tbowowc.com.

The Book of Warfare Weapons
Chapter 14
Prayer of Worship

Prayer of Activation: Father, help me to worship you at all times in spirit and in truth. I love you and always want to worship you in the beauty of holiness. I thank you, Father, that you have given me the grace to worship you through Jesus Christ. The Holy Spirit shall help me to do it effectively for your glory. I thank you for it, Father. In the Name of Jesus Christ, I pray. Amen.

Action: Sing unto the Lord songs that focus on Him and not us. Glorify the Lord in the beauty of holiness. Worship should focus on all He has done, who He is, and all He will yet do. It should magnify the Lord with gratefulness and thanksgiving. The goal should be to draw near to God with a sincere heart.

The Book of Warfare Weapons
Chapter 15
Ministering to the Lord
Primary Purpose: To align with one's purpose
Effective Use: All enemies
Strength: Unlimited

Scriptures:
"As they ministered to the Lord, and fasted, the Holy Ghost said, Separate me Barnabas and Saul for the work whereunto I have called them" (Acts 13:2).

"And she was a widow of about fourscore and four years, which departed not from the temple, but served God with fasting and prayers night and day" (Luke 2:37).

The Attack: You want God to speak to you but don't know how to get Him to do so. You are hungry for a fresh move of God but are tired of all the yokes of religion. You know that there has to be more to God than what you are experiencing, but so many weights are holding you back from pressing into Him.

Weapon of Choice: Ministering to the Lord.

Defensively: This weapon of unlimited power is effective against all the forces of sin, wickedness, and darkness.

Offensively: It allows you to tap into the heavenly realm. The Lord will begin to share secret things with those who love Him and are faithful in using this weapon.

How to Use this Weapon: This is one of the weapons that I use most often. What it does is align a person to their purpose. It's good against all enemies. The revelation is that when a person is Ministering to the Lord, they brag to the Lord about Himself—about what He has done, is doing, or will yet to do in the future. An example is when Moses and Elijah appeared at the Mount of Transfiguration and spoke with Jesus about what He was about to do at Calvary. Another example is in the Book of Acts, where the Bible says they were all Ministering to the Lord and fasted (Acts 13:2).

The Book of Warfare Weapons
Chapter 15
Ministering to the Lord

The challenge is to please the Lord, each day by saying "Lord, how can I make your day? Then be faithfully obedient to do whatsoever the Holy Spirit would lead you to do. By Ministering to the Lord your prayer life will ascend to new heights in God.

Secrets of this Weapon: This weapon is like an excellent spiritual calibrator. It realigns us from focusing on the weaknesses of this life to refocusing on the infinite power of the Giver of Life.

Weapon's Source of Power: This life-changing weapon called Ministering to the Lord is energized by God's love and grace. The love of God fills the believer's heart, and then the believer responds to God out of love and gratitude. It is your way of treating the Lord like who He is—a king. Not just a king, but the "King of Kings." Ministering to the Lord is your time to honor, revere, and express love to Jesus in your special way.

Faith Heroes Using this Weapon: Moses and Elijah on the Mount of Transfiguration (Luke 9:28-31); Abraham (Genesis Chapter 18); Samuel (1 Samuel 2:11, 3:1); Prophetess Ana (Luke 2:36-37); Joshua (Exodus 33:11); Daniel (Daniel 6:10); and many more.

PICK YOUR CHALLENGE: For a more immersive experience pick your challenge below and complete it according to the instructions listed. For the best experience and maximum impact complete all activities, exercises, and challenges.

Your Challenge: Each day, resolve to make the Lord's day by joyfully doing whatever the Holy Spirit would lead you to do.

For A Great Challenge: Complete activities in Chapter #15 of *The Book of Warfare Weapons–Workbook.*

The Book of Warfare Weapons
Chapter 15
Ministering to the Lord

For A Group Challenge: Complete the Group Challenge of Chapter #15 of *The Book of Warfare Weapons–Workbook.*

For A Great Online Challenge: Complete the online activities and challenges in Chapter #15 of *The Book of Warfare Weapons–Outstanding Warrior Challenge (TBOWW-OWC) online challenge at* <u>www.tbowowc.com</u>.

Prayer of Activation: Lord Jesus, there is no one like You. You alone are the King of Kings, Lord of Lords, Prince of Peace, the Word made flesh — the Lamb of God who took away the sins of the world. You are the Self-existing, Holy One of all creation, Maker of Heaven and Earth. You alone, mighty God, defeated Satan, sin, death, Hell, the grave, and all the armies of darkness simultaneously and openly put them to shame. I bless Your glorious Name, for You alone have purchased our salvation with Your Blood. You redeemed us back to our Heavenly Father and gave us the gift of eternal life. Thank You that we will live with You in Your glorious heavenly kingdom. You are indeed worthy, and I count it a joy to minister to You about how great You are. I love You, Jesus Christ. I give You thanksgiving and praise, Holy Father, for allowing me to minister this prayer through the Holy Spirit. I pray it in the Name of Jesus Christ. Amen.

The Book of Warfare Weapons
Chapter 16
Act of Obedience

Primary Purpose: To bring about the blessings of God
Effective Use: Disobedience and rebellion
Strength: Extremely strong

Scriptures:
"And Samuel said, Hath the Lord as great delight in burnt offerings and sacrifices, as in obeying the voice of the Lord? Behold, to obey is better than sacrifice, and to hearken than the fat of rams" (1 Samuel 15:22).
"But he said, *Yea rather, blessed are they that hear the word of God, and keep it*" (Luke 11:28).

The Attack: You desire to do what God tells you to do, but you lack the faith to carry it out. When faced with challenges in life, you often solve them according to your own understanding rather than with the wisdom of the Word of God. You feel that God can bless you even if you don't obey Him because He is a good God and knows your heart. As a result, you find it challenging to do the things that God lays on your heart to do; therefore, you have more excuses than fruit to show for it.

Weapon of Choice: Prayer of Obedience.

Defensively: This mighty weapon is effective against hard-heartedness, disobedience, stubbornness, aborted blessings, doubt, unbelief, pride, arrogance, lies, deceit, tradition, fears, and self-reliance.

Offensively: This mighty weapon is most pleasing to God. Using this weapon will allow you to walk in all the Grace, favor, blessings, anointings, and goodness of God.

How to Use this Weapon: Obedience brings the blessing of God, and it stops the enemy from bringing disobedience and rebellion. The revelation of obedience is that it is proving our love to God by doing what He commands. The manifestation of this was Abraham continually obeying God. The challenge is to ask yourself, "What did God tell you to do, and are you doing it?"

The Book of Warfare Weapons
Chapter 16
Prayer of Act of Obedience

Secrets of this Weapon: In the spirit realm, you are proving your love for God by doing what He commands. It is like all of Heaven is watching to see to what extent you are willing to obey God. It is the highest honor that can ever be bestowed upon a human on earth to be so devoted to obeying God that one would rather die than disobey Him. It is what Jesus did, the three Hebrew boys, Daniel, Stephen, John the Baptist, Paul, Peter, the prophets, and many others (including our Christian brothers and sisters around the world who to this day suffer persecution for their faith in Jesus Christ). For it is written, "If we suffer (*with him*), we shall also reign with him: if we deny him, he also will deny us" (2 Timothy 2:12).

Weapon's Source of Power: This impressive weapon called an Act of Obedience is energized by the love of God. Jesus said, "And why call ye me, Lord, Lord, and do not the things which I say?" (Luke 6:46). Jesus said, "If ye love me, keep my commandments" (John 14:15). True love for God will cause one to obey God. Love has the power to strengthen the believer beyond fear, doubt, insecurity, pride, and weaknesses to fulfill God's will. Obedience is the highest, strongest, and greatest form of worship.

Faith Heroes Using this Weapon: *Jesus is our perfect example (Luke 22:41-43); Abraham (Hebrews 11:8); Mary (Luke 1:38); the eleven apostles (Acts 1:24-26); John the Baptist (John 3:27-30); and Philip (Acts 8:26-27).

PICK YOUR CHALLENGE: For a more immersive experience pick your challenge below and complete it according to the instructions listed.
For the best experience and maximum impact complete all activities, exercises, and challenges.

Your Challenge: What is God telling you to do? Are you doing it?

For A Great Challenge: Complete activities in Chapter #16 of *The Book of Warfare Weapons–Workbook.*

The Book of Warfare Weapons
Chapter 16
Prayer of Act of Obedience

For A Group Challenge: Complete the Group Challenge of Chapter #16 of *The Book of Warfare Weapons–Workbook*.

For A Great Online Challenge: Complete the online activities and challenges in Chapter #16 of *The Book of Warfare Weapons–Outstanding Warrior Challenge (TBOWW-OWC) online challenge* at *www.tbowowc.com*.

Prayer of Activation: Father, thank You so much for giving me the mind of Christ. The Bible says, "Let this mind be in you, which was also in Christ Jesus: Who, being in the form of God, thought it not robbery to be equal with God: But made himself of no reputation, and took upon him the form of a servant, and was made in the likeness of men: And being found in fashion as a man, he humbled himself and became obedient unto death, even the death of the cross" (Philippians 2:5-8). Help me to overcome disobedience and rebellion and to follow Your will completely. Help me surrender my self-will—"not my will, but Thine will be done" (Luke 22:42)—and seek Your perfect will in every area of my life. Through faith and the empowerment of your Holy Spirit, I thank you that You have enabled me to walk in obedience unto You this day. By faith, I shall do it to the praise and honor of Your glory, Father. In the Name of Jesus Christ, I pray. Amen.

The Book of Warfare Weapons
Chapter 17
Prayer of Unity

Primary Purpose: To release the combined strength of numbers
Effective Use: Isolation and rebellion
Strength: Very strong

Scriptures:

"Endeavoring to keep the unity of the Spirit in the bond of peace" (Ephesians 4:3).

"Now I beseech you, brethren, by the name of our Lord Jesus Christ, that ye all speak the same thing, and that there be no divisions among you; but that ye be perfectly joined together in the same mind and in the same judgment" (1 Corinthians 1:10).

The Attack: You are tired of being around people. You don't like to fellowship with other Christians, and you don't see the need to attend church. You feel that God can speak to you Himself, and therefore you do not submit yourself to anyone as a spiritual covering or pastor. You act like a lone ranger in the spirit realm and are accountable to no one. You would rather watch "church" on TV than attend a live gathering. You think there are too many hypocrites in the church and that you are the only one trying to live right.

Weapon of Choice: Prayer of Unity.

Defensively: This powerful weapon is effective against discord, confusion, sabotage, division, diversions, distractions, isolation, error, heresies, loneliness, false doctrines, and deceptions.

Offensively: Using this weapon connects you to power that continually increases and multiplies each time you join with other believers.

How to Use this Weapon: The superiority of this revelation shows the intentional fellowship of love against all opposition. A perfect manifestation is Nehemiah building the wall. They stayed together in unity and continued to build in the midst of those trying to bring discouragement and delay. A wall that should have taken years to rebuild was rebuilt through the power of unity in only 52 days.

The Book of Warfare Weapons
Chapter 17
Prayer of Unity

Your life will also experience wonderous rebuilding through committing to unity. Now, what challenges of unity are you experiencing? Are you a part of a church? If not, why not? And what can you do to make sure you have church unity with your fellow believers?

Secrets of this Weapon: In the spirit realm, it is like a person has taken their reserved seat in heavenly places of the congregation of the righteous, on Mount Zion, sides of the north, city of the Great King (Psalms 48:2). The power of the divine unity of God is released each time a person participates in the unity of fellowship by faith (1 John 5:7, Ephesians 2:6, and Psalm 48:1-2).

Weapon's Source of Power: This mighty weapon called Prayer of Unity is energized by the divine unity of God. Jesus prayed to the Father to include us in the divine unity and fellowship of love. "*That they all may be one; as thou, Father, art in me, and I in thee, that they also may be one in us: that the world may believe that thou hast sent me*" *(John 17:21)*.

Faith Heroes Using this Weapon: Nehemiah rebuilding the wall (Nehemiah 8:1-7); Moses (Exodus 12:37, 51); David (2 Samuel 6:1-5); Josiah (2 Kings 23:1-2); King Solomon (1 Kings 8:1-5); and many more.

PICK YOUR CHALLENGE: For a more immersive experience pick your challenge below and complete it according to the instructions listed.
For the best experience and maximum impact complete all activities, exercises, and challenges.

Your Challenge: Are you part of a church? If not, why not? Allow the Holy Spirit to lead you to one.

For A Great Challenge: Complete activities in Chapter #17 of *The Book of Warfare Weapons–Workbook.*

The Book of Warfare Weapons
Chapter 17
Prayer of Unity

For A Group Challenge: Complete the Group Challenge of Chapter #17 of *The Book of Warfare Weapons–Workbook.*

For A Great Online Challenge: Complete the online activities and challenges in Chapter #17 of *The Book of Warfare Weapons–Outstanding Warrior Challenge (TBOWW-OWC) challenge at* www.tbowowc.com.

Prayer of Activation: Father, I thank You that, through Your Holy Spirit, we can stay together in unity. Thank You, dear God, for making it possible for me to have fellowship with my fellow brethren and attend a church where I continually receive the Word of God. Please help me, through the Holy Spirit, to always seek to be in unity. Help me overcome all forces, ideas, thoughts, or perceptions that would cause me to be isolated or walk in disobedience. Thus, I receive the strength of God to walk in complete obedience and submission to You, and to fulfill Your will. May I continue to endeavor to keep the unity of the Spirit, and the bond of peace, through the Holy Spirit. In the Name of Jesus Christ, I pray. Amen.

The Book of Warfare Weapons
Chapter 18
High Praises
Primary Purpose: To bring deliverance
Effective Use: Send ambushments
Strength: Very strong

Scriptures:
"Let the high praises of God be in their mouth, and a two-edged sword in their hand; To execute vengeance upon the heathen, and punishment upon the people; To bind their kings with chains, and their nobles with fetters of iron; To execute upon them the judgment written: this honor have all his saints. Praise ye the Lord" (Psalm 149:6-9).

"Glory to God in the highest, and on earth peace, good will toward men" (Luke 2:14).

The Attack: You feel like crying. Intense pressure is crushing you. You feel as if you are about to break. You don't know how much more you can take. You feel like giving up. Your situation appears bleak. The enemy keeps telling you that you are going to fail. You just received bad news. There are many more reasons, too numerous to list in their entirety.

Weapon of Choice: High Praises.

Defensively: This weapon is effective against spiritual attacks, captivity, bondage, threats, oppression, and injustices.

Offensively: Praise, honor, reverence, and greatly please God. Praise puts God first, and it terrorizes the enemy. The use of this weapon will send ambush attacks against the enemy's camp. It will also execute vengeance and judgment against the enemy, even to the point of binding their evil kings in chains, and their evil principalities in fetters of iron.

How to Use this Weapon: High Praises are faith-filled praises outside of one's comfort zone. High Praises are offered loudly. So it is when you are praising God, and you don't care how you look, or what people say. You're in warfare, you're in the Spirit, and you're doing battle. You begin to praise God with such faith that it takes you out of your comfort zone.

The Book of Warfare Weapons
Chapter 18
High Praises

The manifestation of this is in 2 Chronicles 20 and 22, where God sent ambushments against the enemy. The challenge is to send up High Praises each day. High Praises cause the devil to experience intense anguish and sudden desperation each time a believer engages in them.

Secrets of this Weapon: It is like a shout of faith that releases explosive victory in the spirit realm. This shout of faith activates the working of miracles, signs, and wonders. The way a crystal glass can shatter on earth if one hits the right, high-pitch frequency, so can things be shattered with high praise. High praise is extreme faith that is proclaimed to bring victory. High praise is so potent that it can only be released in a shout! Praise the Lord!!! High praise terrorizes the devil, for each time it is released, the enemy faces defeat.

Weapon's Source of Power: This mighty weapon called High Praises is energized by the goodness of God. There is a place within the soul of every person that is reserved for God alone. When a person allows that reserved place to be filled with the goodness of God, shouts of high praise come ringing out! "Command your soul to bless the Lord and let High Praises flow!" (Psalm 103:1-2).

Faith Heroes Using this Weapon: God sent ambushments (2 Chronicles 20-22); Joshua (Joshua 6:20); Jacob and Israel (Numbers 23:21); Israel bringing the ark (1 Samuel 4:5-7); David (Psalm 47:1-6); Gideon (Judges 7:20); Judah (2 Chronicles 13:15); Israel on Palm Sunday (John 12:13); future saints (Revelation 19:6); and many others.

PICK YOUR CHALLENGE: For a more immersive experience pick your challenge below and complete it according to the instructions listed.
For the best experience and maximum impact complete all activities, exercises, and challenges.

Your Challenge: Terrorize the enemy by offering up continual High Praises to God.

The Book of Warfare Weapons
Chapter 18
Prayer of High Praises

For A Great Challenge: Complete activities in Chapter #18 of *The Book of Warfare Weapons–Workbook.*

For A Group Challenge: Complete the Group Challenge of Chapter #18 of *The Book of Warfare Weapons–Workbook.*

For A Great Online Challenge: Complete the online activities and challenges in Chapter #18 of *The Book of Warfare Weapons–Outstanding Warrior Challenge (TBOWW-OWC) online challenge at* www.tbowowc.com.

Prayer of Activation: Hallelujah!!!! God, You are worthy!!! There is none like You, Lord! Glory to Your Name!!! How excellent You are, mighty God! Wonderful Counselor! Jesus, You are amazing!!! Thank You, Holy Spirit, for being in my life!!! Thank You, God, for making all things possible! Praise the Lord! I love You, God! I love You, Jesus! I love You, Holy Spirit! Hallelujah! Glory, honor, dominion, power, grace, mercy, strength, and wisdom belong to our God!!! Bless Your Holy Name! I offer You this High Praise through the Holy Spirit! May it please You and bring You honor and glory!!! May Your name be praised forever!!! In the Name of Jesus Christ, I pray. Amen!!!

The Book of Warfare Weapons
Chapter 19
Mercy
Primary Purpose: To withhold judgment
Effective Use: All enemies and all things
Strength: Divine class

Scripture:
"And he said, I will make all my goodness pass before thee, and I will proclaim the name of the Lord before thee; and will be gracious to whom I will be gracious, and will shew mercy on whom I will shew mercy" (Exodus 33:19).

The Attack: You have offended or trespassed, and you are about to receive judgment. You messed up "big," and now you must face the consequences. Someone has offended you, and you now have the chance to get revenge. The fortune of someone who did you wrong now rests in your hands.

Weapon of Choice: Mercy.

Defensively: This weapon is excellent for intercepting, canceling, withholding, withdrawing, and destroying judgment. It is also effective against bitterness, unforgiveness, meanness, violence, revenge, hatred, and condemnation.

Offensively: The continual use of this weapon will cause you to be flooded with Mercy. Compassion will surround you like a shield.

How to Use this Weapon: You request that judgment be withheld because of the goodness of God. A person can also grant Mercy instead of judgment to anyone who has offended them. You can receive it, and you can offer it to others. Compassion is Mercy—helping one who is afflicted or has suffered a loss. The enemy enjoys seeing people condemned, judged, and punished. God loves to see people faultless, acquitted, and pardoned. God loves to see people who truly learn from their mistakes and go on to live better lives. God desires to give Mercy instead of judgment. God wants us to receive His Mercy and to give it freely to others.

The Book of Warfare Weapons
Chapter 19
Prayer of Mercy

Secrets of this Weapon: In the spirit realm, it is like you have received a court order that says you are guilty and should be punished. Then, the supreme court comes to overrule the lower court's order by declaring that punishment is set aside or annulled because of Jesus Christ giving you a pardon. Mercy removes judgment. Mercy is like giving a person another chance even when they don't deserve it. Mercy is a spiritual thing that combines God's love, goodness, and Grace to help us.

Weapon's Source of Power: This divine weapon of Mercy is energized by the love, goodness, and gentleness of God. Mercy is often accompanied by Grace. Mercy and Grace both receive authority and power from God's love.

Faith Heroes Using this Weapon: *Jesus is our perfect example (John 8:3-11); Rahab (Joshua 2:4); The Good Samaritan (Luke 10:25-37); King Solomon (1 Kings 2:36-37); David (1 Samuel 24:1-7); Elisha (2 Kings 6:20-23); Abigail (1 Samuel 25:14-35); and many others.

PICK YOUR CHALLENGE: For a more immersive experience pick your challenge below and complete it according to the instructions listed.
For the best experience and maximum impact complete all activities, exercises, and challenges.

Your Challenge: See how many people you can show Mercy to this week.

For A Great Challenge: Complete activities in Chapter #19 of *The Book of Warfare Weapons–Workbook.*

For A Group Challenge: Complete the Group Challenge of Chapter #19 of *The Book of Warfare Weapons–Workbook.*

Chapter 19
Prayer of Mercy

For A Great Online Challenge: Complete the online activities and challenges in Chapter #19 of *The Book of Warfare Weapons—Outstanding Warrior Challenge (TBOWW-OWC) online challenge at* <u>www.tbowowc.com</u>.

Prayer of Activation: Father, I thank You for showing me Mercy. Thank You that through Your Mercy, You have delivered me from the prison, purpose, power, and penalty of sin. Father, you desire that I show Mercy to others, as I have received Mercy from You. I release my faith to receive power, by Your Holy Spirit, to receive Mercy from You freely. I believe that You have also empowered me to show Mercy to others by Your Grace. I confess that I have power from You to show Mercy to others. I declare that I shall freely give Mercy to all who need it through the Holy Spirit. I thank You for helping me to do it, Father, for Your glory. In the Name of Jesus Christ, I pray. Amen.

The Book of Warfare Weapons
Chapter 20
Grace

Primary Purpose: To obtain unmerited favor/ability from God
Effective Use: All enemies and all things
Strength: Divine class

Scripture:
"Let us therefore come boldly unto the throne of grace, that we may obtain mercy, and find grace to help in time of need" (Hebrews 4:16).

The Attack: You want to receive some good thing from God, but you don't feel worthy to receive it. You are under attack by thoughts of fear, doubt, and unbelief. You want to excel in the things of God, but your past weaknesses, inadequacies, or works are holding you back. You feel that you can never be good enough to please God. You often find yourself asking God, "Please don't pass me by," or, "Please don't leave me."

Weapon of Choice: Grace.

Defensively: This weapon is so powerful that it is in the divine class and is effective against all enemies and all things.

Offensively: It allows you to receive all the blessings and goodness of God through Jesus Christ.

How to Use this Weapon: God wraps all His goodness, mercy, and love into a spiritual element called Grace. It is a substance that causes God to choose you as the recipient of His overflowing goodness. Grace is God's favor that He gives without you having to work to earn it. Therefore, it is known as "unmerited," which means it is not based on how good or bad you are. Grace is like a coin with two sides. The front side is unmerited favor. The backside is the strength of God flowing through an individual, helping him to succeed.

Secrets of this Weapon: In the spirit realm, you have been chosen to receive all the goodness of God, not because you are good, but because He is good. The goodness of God moves Him to release goodness at all times. He looks for someone to whom He can lavish with His goodness.

The Book of Warfare Weapons
Chapter 20
Prayer of Grace

Grace is the spiritual method that He uses to expose the whole world to His goodness. Jesus is the point-person to administer all the Grace of God. For it is written, "For the law was given by Moses, but grace and truth came by Jesus Christ" (John 1:17). Grace has already chosen you to experience all of His goodness, but you must legally accept it by faith to benefit from it.

Weapon's Source of Power: This divine weapon of Grace is energized by the love, goodness, and gentleness of God. Grace is often accompanied by Mercy. Grace and Mercy both receive authority and power from God's love.

Faith Heroes Using this Weapon: *Jesus is our perfect example of Grace (Ephesians 2:8-9, 4:7); Queen Esther received it (Esther 2:16-17); Stephen (Acts 6:8); David to Mephibosheth (2 Samuel 9:7-13); Noah (Genesis 6:8); and many more.

PICK YOUR CHALLENGE: For a more immersive experience pick your challenge below and complete it according to the instructions listed.
For the best experience and maximum impact complete all activities, exercises, and challenges.

Your Challenge: Ask God to give you more Grace today.

For A Great Challenge: Complete activities in Chapter #20 of *The Book of Warfare Weapons–Workbook.*

For A Group Challenge: Complete the Group Challenge of Chapter #20 of *The Book of Warfare Weapons–Workbook.*

For A Great Online Challenge: Complete the online activities and challenges in Chapter #20 of *The Book of Warfare Weapons–Outstanding Warrior Challenge (TBOWW-OWC)* online challenge at *www.tbowowc.com*

The Book of Warfare Weapons
Chapter 20
Prayer of Grace

Prayer of Activation: Father, thank You for loving the world so much that You gave Your only begotten Son to die on the cross so that we may have eternal life. Thank You for giving me Grace freely and abundantly so that it is running over. Thank You that it is by Grace, through faith, I can receive all the blessings of Heaven, as they come through Jesus Christ. Please teach me to always trust in Your Grace rather than in my own ability. I thank You, Father, for Your Grace flows to me through the Holy Spirit. In the Name of Jesus Christ, I pray. Amen.

The Book of Warfare Weapons
Chapter 21
Spiritual Songs
Primary Purpose: God-directed prophecy in music
Effective Use: Many enemies
Strength: Very strong

Scriptures:
"Speaking to yourselves in psalms and hymns and spiritual songs, singing and making melody in your heart to the Lord" (Ephesians 5:19).
"Let the word of Christ dwell in you richly in all wisdom; teaching and admonishing one another in psalms and hymns and spiritual songs, singing with grace in your hearts to the Lord" (Colossians 3:16).

The Attack: You feel exhausted, physically and spiritually, then you receive bad news. You feel like letting out a scream because of all the mounting pressure. You think to yourself, "Where are you, God? Do you care if I perish?"

Weapon of Choice: Spiritual Songs.

Defensively: This mighty weapon is effective against all personal struggles and challenges of life. It often comes as evidence that one has received the victory: therefore, it is known as a "victory song."

Offensively: The use of this weapon will help you to stay full of the joy, peace, and faith of God. The continual use of this weapon will also help you access the "mysteries of God"—prophecy, boldness, confidence, understanding—and will help you change levels in the spirit.

How to Use this Weapon: It is God's directed prophecy in music. It's effective against many enemies. The revelation is a new song to God, led by the Holy Spirit, and sung from one's own spirit. It's a brand-new song a person sings from their spirit that they have never heard before. The manifestation is the angels in revelation singing a new song unto God. The challenge to the people is to make the Lord a new song, or sing unto the Lord a brand-new song from your heart, and sing it by faith.

The Book of Warfare Weapons
Chapter 21
Prayer for Spiritual Songs

Secrets of this Weapon: In the spirit realm, it is as if you are listening to music coming directly from Heaven (usually as angelic worship). Then at other times, it is as if God has birthed a new song from the fertile soil of your heart for Him.

Weapon's Source of Power: The mighty weapon called spirit songs is energized by the Holy Spirit. When activated, it's the love of God overflowing from a grateful heart while under the Holy Spirit's anointing. It's a new song flowing from the Throne of God.

Faith Heroes Using this Weapon: Moses (Exodus 15:1); Prophetess Miriam (Exodus 15:20-21); Prophetess Deborah and Barak (Judges 5:1-31); the Levites and priests (Ezra 3:11); Isaiah (Isaiah Chapter 5); future saints (Revelation 5:9, 14:3, 15:3, 19:1-6); David (Psalm 96); and many more.

PICK YOUR CHALLENGE: For a more immersive experience pick your challenge below and complete it according to the instructions listed.
For the best experience and maximum impact complete all activities, exercises, and challenges.

Your Challenge: Offer the Lord a new song from your heart.

For A Great Challenge: Complete activities in Chapter #21 of *The Book of Warfare Weapons–Workbook.*

For A Group Challenge: Complete the Group Challenge of Chapter #21 of *The Book of Warfare Weapons–Workbook.*

For A Great Online Challenge: Complete the online activities and challenges in Chapter #21 of *The Book of Warfare Weapons–Outstanding Warrior Challenge (TBOWW-OWC) online challenge at* www.tbowowc.com.

The Book of Warfare Weapons
Chapter 21
Prayer for Spiritual Songs

Prayer of Activation: Father, I thank You for the finished work of Jesus Christ. I thank You that He purchased for us all the blessings of Heaven. I thank You that one of the heavenly blessings is spirit songs. Father, I ask that through the enablement of Your Holy Spirit, You would sing through me. I ask that You allow a song that I will sing in psalms, hymns, and Spiritual Songs, singing and making melody in my heart unto You. Let the Holy Spirit teach me and guide me in the words of that spirit song. Let my spirit always be in a state of worshipping You. May I be faithful to bless Your Name from deep within the heart of my spirit. May I always have a spirit song that will come forth. May I sing it to bring praise, honor, and glory to Your wonderful Name. I thank You, Father, for giving me spirit songs through the Holy Spirit. I believe that I receive them. I look forward to having them manifest to glorify Jesus Christ. In the Name of Jesus Christ, I pray. Amen.

The Book of Warfare Weapons
Chapter 22
Spiritual Tongues
Primary Purpose: To access the mysteries of Heaven
Effective Use: Many uses
Strength: Extremely strong

Scriptures:

"And they were all filled with the Holy Ghost, and began to speak with other tongues, as the Spirit gave them utterance" (Acts 2:4).

"For he that speaketh in an unknown tongue speaketh not unto men, but unto God: for no man understandeth him; howbeit in the Spirit he speaketh mysteries" (1 Corinthians 14:2).

The Attack: You know you should pray, but you don't feel like it. You try to pray but can't think of anything to say. You try to think of a Bible verse, but nothing comes to mind. You realize that you are praying less often than before. You are facing an urgent life crisis but don't know how to pray about it the right way.

Weapon of Choice: Spiritual Tongues.

Defensively: This mighty weapon is effective against doubt, fear, confusion, unbelief, spiritual attacks, hindrances to prayer, religion, tradition, worry, anxiety, oppression, depression, sabotage, evil powers and plans, division, weakness, danger, trouble, and many more.

Offensively: This weapon is also a spiritual gift. Its primary use is to access the mysteries of Heaven. It is revealed as the gift of speaking in heavenly languages. One of the most significant benefits of this weapon (and spiritual gift) is that it is a spiritual language given by the Holy Spirit, that allows you to communicate directly with the Father, through Jesus Christ. It is a language that the devil doesn't know or understand because it was created specifically by the Father for those who are children of God by redemption. Spiritual tongues are usually the first sign that one has received the baptism in the Holy Spirit. It usually manifests when: praying directly to God from the spirit, transitioning from natural prayer to spiritual prayer, and speaking mysteries into existence.

The Book of Warfare Weapons
Chapter 22
Prayer for Spiritual Tongues

How to Use this Weapon: The manifestation is that it appeared on the day of Pentecost in Acts Chapter 2. The challenge is for people to believe in it and begin to pray in tongues every day.

Secrets of this Weapon: In the spirit realm, a believer has activated his faith to speak in his "new birth" heavenly language. This language gives him or her access to divine blessings, wisdom, and power beyond human understanding. The Holy Spirit is the one who gives, activates, directs, and teaches us knowledge about this spiritual gift and weapon.

Weapon's Source of Power: The spiritual gift and incredible weapon called Spiritual Tongues, unknown tongues, or simply tongues, is energized by the power of the Holy Spirit Baptism. Speaking in tongues was the one sign that the apostles and early church accepted as a sign from God that the person had received the Baptism in the Holy Spirit (Acts 10:44-46).

Faith Heroes Using this Weapon: Saints on the Day of Pentecost (Acts 2:1-4); Peter (Acts 2:14-20); Cornelius and his household (Acts 10: 44-46); Saints at church at Corinth (1 Corinthians Chapter 14); Paul (1 Corinthians 14:18); Jude (Jude 1:20); and many more.

PICK YOUR CHALLENGE: For a more immersive experience pick your challenge below and complete it according to the instructions listed.
For the best experience and maximum impact complete all activities, exercises, and challenges.

Your Challenge: Believe for it and receive it by faith. Pray in tongues each day.

For A Great Challenge: Complete activities in Chapter #22 of *The Book of Warfare Weapons—Workbook*.

The Book of Warfare Weapons
Chapter 22
Prayer for Spiritual Tongues

For A Group Challenge: Complete the Group Challenge of Chapter #22 of *The Book of Warfare Weapons–Workbook*.

For A Great Online Challenge: Complete the online activities and challenges in Chapter #22 of *The Book of Warfare Weapons–Outstanding Warrior Challenge (TBOWW-OWC) challenge at www.tbowowc.com*.

Prayer of Activation: Father, I thank You that by Your Grace, I have access to Spiritual Tongues. This gift comes as proof that Jesus Christ has been glorified, and He has sent the Holy Spirit. Thank You that I have received an unbroken, direct channel to speak to You, Father God. And when I speak in the Spirit, it's a mystery, but the Holy Spirit then converts my words and makes them known—even the hidden mysteries and the wisdom of God. I thank You that Spiritual Tongues of the Holy Spirit are a sign and that You use them to manifest the fullness of Your will and to reveal the mysteries of Heaven. May Your Holy Spirit always pray through me in tongues. May I operate in it continually, praying in tongues that Your divine will be done. I give You thanks and praise, Father. I believe that I will begin to operate in it by the Holy Spirit. In the Name of Jesus Christ, I pray. Amen.

The Book of Warfare Weapons
Chapter 23
Interpretation of Tongues
Primary Purpose: To see the mysteries of Heaven revealed
Effective Use: Many enemies
Strength: Extremely strong

Scriptures:
"To another the workings of miracles; to another prophecy; to another discerning of spirits; to another divers kinds of tongues; to another the interpretation of tongues" (1 Corinthians 12:10).

"How is it then, brethren? When ye come together, every one of you hath a psalm, hath a doctrine, hath a tongue, hath a revelation, hath an interpretation. Let all things be done unto edifying" (1 Corinthians 14:26).

The Attack: Someone has spoken in tongues, and you wonder if it is really from the Lord. Someone has spoken in tongues, but no one in the church knows what it means. Everybody is waiting for someone to interpret the message in the native language of the hearers, but no one steps forward. You wish you knew the message, but you dare not say anything because you may be wrong.

Weapon of Choice: Interpretation of Tongues.

Defensively: This powerful weapon is effective against confusion, chaos, division, deception, fear, doubt, shame, ridicule, oppression, heaviness, anxiety, stress, calamity, disaster, misfortune, tradition, religion, pride, peer pressure, schemes, and rebellion.

Offensively: This weapon is also a spiritual gift that reveals the mind of God. It can take the whole congregation to new levels of anointing in the spirit realm in just a moment of time. It ushers in the peace, power, and presence of God. When activated to interpret a message of tongues, it operates on the same level as prophecy.

How to Use this Weapon: Someone spoke a message in tongues, and the message in tongues needs to be supernaturally interpreted into a message understood in English (or the native language of listeners).

The Book of Warfare Weapons
Chapter 23
Prayer for Interpretation of Tongues

Its primary use is to reveal the mysteries of Heaven. It's good against all enemies. It is the gift of interpreting spiritual tongues (which are mysteries) and clearly and accurately sharing their meaning (uncovering the mystery) in one's native language through the anointing of the Holy Spirit. The manifestation is Paul's speaking about it, and the challenge is to ask God to allow it to flow through you or ask God for it.

Secrets of this Weapon: In the spirit realm, God enlightens one with spiritual understanding to the point that the Spirit is empowered to comprehend what is spoken, written, dreamed, or seen in the spirit realm. This grace to comprehend, understand, and interpret spiritual languages and mysteries is a spiritual gift administered by the Holy Spirit. It also allows one to interpret dreams, visions, signs, wonders, mysteries, and secrets of the heart.

Weapon's Source of Power: This mighty weapon called Interpretation of Tongues is a spiritual gift as well as a spiritual weapon. The power of the Holy Spirit energizes the Interpretation of Tongues.

Faith Heroes Using this Weapon: People witnessed its power (Acts 2:6-11); Paul taught its proper operation (1 Corinthians 14: 26-28); Daniel (Daniel Chapter 5); and others.

PICK YOUR CHALLENGE: For a more immersive experience pick your challenge below and complete it according to the instructions listed. For the best experience and maximum impact complete all activities, exercises, and challenges.

Your Challenge: Pray and ask God for the Gift of Interpretation of Tongues.

For A Great Challenge: Complete activities in Chapter #23 of *The Book of Warfare Weapons–Workbook.*

The Book of Warfare Weapons
Chapter 23
Prayer for Interpretation of Tongues

For A Group Challenge: Complete the Group Challenge of Chapter #23 of *The Book of Warfare Weapons–Workbook.*

For A Great Online Challenge: Complete the online activities and the challenges in Chapter #23 of *The Book of Warfare Weapons–Outstanding Warrior Challenge (TBOWW-OWC) online challenge at* www.tbowowc.com.

Prayer of Activation: Father, I thank You so much for giving me the interpretation of tongues. I thank You that this gift comprehends spiritual tongues and converts them into a language that can be understood in the native language. Father, I pray by Your Grace, let this gift operate in me. I pray that as I begin to speak in tongues, or as others around me speak in tongues, the Holy Spirit would interpret it. Father, I believe that this is a grace that You've given us due to the finished work of Jesus Christ and the Baptism of the Holy Spirit. I release my faith to operate in it now. I believe that I receive by faith. I declare that it shall manifest to the praise and honor of Your Glory by the Holy Spirit. I thank You for it, Father. In the Name of Jesus Christ, I pray. Amen.

The Book of Warfare Weapons
Chapter 24
Discerning of Spirits
Primary Purpose: To detect spiritual beings
Effective Use: Deception
Strength: Extremely strong

Scriptures:

"To another the workings of miracles; to another prophecy; to another discerning of spirits; to another divers kinds of tongues; to another the interpretation of tongues" (1 Corinthians 12:10).

"But Peter said, Ananias, why hath Satan filled thine heart to lie to the Holy Ghost, and to keep back part of the price of the land?" (Acts 5:3).

The Attack: Someone with smooth words comes in with the intent to deceive, supplant, or take advantage of you or others. Someone comes presenting themselves as being from God, but you aren't sure. You wish there were some way you could, with 100% accuracy, identify if they are abiding in the truth before that person has caused hurt, harm, or damage.

Weapon of Choice: Discerning of Spirits.

Defensively: This weapon is also a spiritual gift. It is effective against deception, masquerades, secrets, plots and schemes, witches, sorcery, magic, spells, curses, cruelty, manipulation, possessions, intimidation, soul-ties, evil contracts and covenants, principalities, powers, rulers of the darkness, and spiritual wickedness in high places.

Offensively: This weapon (gift) helps to protect the Church and individuals from being deceived. This weapon empowers individuals to recognize the difference between holy angels, human spirits, and unholy spirits. This gift also reveals the truth concerning the root of any issue and whatever entity may be causing a challenge. It gives precise answers to issues with pinpoint accuracy. It also allows one to witness events, either by seeing, hearing, or visiting (through visions and dreams, as the Holy Spirits leads), the actual event in the past, present, or future to reveal the mind of God.

The Book of Warfare Weapons
Chapter 24
Prayer for Discerning of Spirits

How to Use this Weapon: Its primary use is discerning the presence of spiritual beings. It is effective against deception. The revelation is the gift to detect different spirits and their nature. The manifestation is Peter to Ananias, and Simon, the ex-sorcerer, as he could detect the true intent of their hearts. It also clarifies when a true prophet and a false prophet give contradictory prophecies to people on the same matter (1 Kings Chapter 22).

Secrets of this Weapon: In the spirit realm, this weapon helps to protect against deception. A person with this spiritual gift would, on occasion, see angels or demons as God wills it. The person may also see the human spirit and the type of spirit that binds it or possesses it. This spiritual gift is an outstanding weapon for use in deliverance.

Weapon's Source of Power: This spiritual gift and powerful weapon called Discerning of Spirits is energized by the power of the Holy Spirit.

Faith Heroes Using this Weapon: Micaiah (1 Kings Chapter 22); Peter to Ananias and Sapphira (Acts 5:1-11); Peter to Simon the ex-sorcerer (Acts 8:9-24); Nehemiah (Nehemiah 6:10-12); Paul (Acts 13:6-12); John (1 John 4:1-3); and many others.

PICK YOUR CHALLENGE: For a more immersive experience pick your challenge below and complete it according to the instructions listed.
For the best experience and maximum impact complete all activities, exercises, and challenges.

Your Challenge: How would your life be different if you operated in Discerning of Spirits at all times? Pray to do so
.

For A Great Challenge: Complete activities in Chapter #24 of *The Book of Warfare Weapons–Workbook.*

Chapter 24
Prayer for Discerning of Spirits

For A Group Challenge: Complete the Group Challenge of Chapter #24 of *The Book of Warfare Weapons–Workbook.*

For A Great Online Challenge: Complete the online activities and challenges in Chapter #24 of *The Book of Warfare Weapons–Outstanding Warrior Challenge (TBOWW-OWC) challenge at* <u>www.tbowowc.com.</u>

Prayer of Activation: Father, thank You for giving us the gift of the Discerning of Spirits. It is a spiritual gift of the Holy Spirit by which we can detect what is of You, God, what is of human origin, and what is of demonic origin. God, I pray that You'll allow this gift You've given to the body of Christ to flow and operate in me. May the Holy Spirit use this gift in me. May I grow in wisdom and Discerning of Spirits to fully utilize the gift for Your Glory. For Your Word says Your sheep hear Your voice, and a stranger they will not follow. I believe that I receive this tremendous spiritual gift through the Holy Spirit. I thank You, for it Father. In the Name of Jesus Christ, I pray. Amen.

The Book of Warfare Weapons
Chapter 25
Prophecy
Primary Purpose: Spirit of Revelation
Effective Use: Many enemies
Strength: Extremely strong

Scriptures:
"Knowing this first, that no prophecy of the scripture is of any private interpretation. For the prophecy came not in old time by the will of man: but holy men of God spake as they were moved by the Holy Ghost" (2 Peter 1:20-21). "And as he spake by the mouth of his holy prophets, which have been since the world began" (Luke 1:70).

The Attack: You are at a crossroads in life and don't know which way to go. You wish God would send a specific word that would speak directly to your situation or life circumstance. You wish there were some way you could know the specific mind of God for your life.

Weapon of Choice: Prophecy.

Defensively: This weapon is effective against all enemies.

Offensively: This weapon is also a spiritual gift. It can speak forth a direct, unrehearsed, fresh message from God in Heaven and reveal His mind concerning a specific matter. It can release judgment and vengeance against the enemy. But it can also release faith, hope, peace, joy, wisdom, understanding, direction, healing, deliverance, recovery, strength, confidence, increase, opportunity, promotion, victory, and breakthrough in mere seconds.

How to Use this Weapon: Its primary purpose is the Spirit of revelation. A person with it can understand the things of God as He either speak through that person or reveals things that are hidden mysteries in the Spirit. The manifestation is the prophet Agabus and how he was able to prophesy that there would be a famine coming to the land. Everybody was able to respond accordingly, and many other scriptures support that as well. The challenge is knowing what to do with a prophesy you receive, how to wait for its appointed time, and how to shift in faith to live it out.

The Book of Warfare Weapons
Chapter 25
Prayer for Prophecy

Secrets of this Weapon: In the spirit realm, Prophecy is as if a person has received top-security clearance in Heaven. The clearance has allowed them to have access to top-secret information that comes from the divine wisdom of God. The person has access to this realm of information as they open their mouth in faith to declare what God has revealed to them.

Weapon's Source of Power: This spiritual gift and special weapon called Prophecy is energized by the Holy Spirit. Prophecies flow on different levels. There is an unlimited number of levels in God. And on each level, there are various measures, powers, authorities, and anointings; therefore, no two prophets are ever alike. The ministry of each person within the gift of Prophecy is unique and original. A person can flow in levels of Prophecy without being a prophet or prophetess. The highest levels of Prophecy are reserved for those God places in the office of the prophet. Therefore, every person should prophesy according to their proportion of faith (Romans 12:6).

Faith Heroes Using this Weapon: Deborah (Judges 4:4-7); Agabus (Acts 11:27-30); A man of God (1 Kings Chapter 13); Haggai and Zechariah (Ezra 5:1-2,14); Ezekiel (Ezekiel 25:1-7); Jeremiah (Jeremiah Chapters 1-2); and many others.

PICK YOUR CHALLENGE: For a more immersive experience pick your challenge below and complete it according to the instructions listed.
For the best experience and maximum impact complete all activities, exercises, and challenges.

Your Challenge: What should you do with Prophecy? Ask God to allow the gift of Prophecy to flow through you.

For A Great Challenge: Complete activities in Chapter #25 of *The Book of Warfare Weapons—Workbook.*

The Book of Warfare Weapons
Chapter 25
Prayer for Prophecy

For A Group Challenge: Complete the Group Challenge of Chapter #25 of *The Book of Warfare Weapons–Workbook.*

For A Great Online Challenge: Complete the online activities and challenges in Chapter #25 of *The Book of Warfare Weapons–Outstanding Warrior Challenge (TBOWW-OWC) online challenge at* www.tbowowc.com

.

Prayer of Activation: Father, I thank You for giving us the gift of Prophecy, by which we can prophesy according to the power of Your Holy Spirit. Prophecy is one of the best gifts that Your Word says we should desire. This gift edifies the whole church, rather than just the individual. Because You said we should desire this gift, I pray that You would allow it to operate in me. Help me to flow in it continually and to increase in it. May Your divine will be fulfilled through its use and operation. Teach me, by Your Holy Spirit, how to flow in prophecy. Teach me how to accept it, how to look for it, and how to operate in it to the praise and honor of Your Glory. I believe that I have received it through the Holy Spirit. I thank You, Father, for it. In the Name of Jesus Christ, I pray. Amen.

The Book of Warfare Weapons
Chapter 26
Word of Wisdom

Primary Purpose: Reveals future events
Effective Use: Many enemies
Strength: Very strong

Scriptures: "For to one is given by the Spirit the word of wisdom; to another the word of knowledge by the same Spirit" (1 Corinthians 12:8). "For the Lord giveth wisdom: out of his mouth cometh knowledge and understanding" (Proverbs 2:6).

The Attack: You must make a major decision concerning an area of your life, but you don't know what to do or which way to go. If only God would reveal to you what the future holds concerning the matter. Doubt, worry, anxiety, fear, lack of concentration, images of defeat, and embarrassment begin to harass you because you don't know what to do.

Weapon of Choice: Word of Wisdom.

Defensively: This powerful weapon is also a spiritual gift and is effective against many enemies. It is especially effective against worry, fears, anxiety, confusion, mistakes, presumption, embarrassment, shame, failures, defeat, ignorance, foolishness, pride, and deception.

Offensively: This weapon helps to bring direction, instruction, truth, clarity, revelation, safety, victory, truth, wisdom, knowledge, and peace.

Important Notes for this Weapon: The weapon (and spiritual gift) of the Word of Wisdom reveals the heart and the mind of God. When in operation, the weapon accesses knowledge of future events before they occur. A perfect example of its manifestation was in the prophet Samuel, who spoke about specific events before they occurred, including even the most delicate details of what would happen. For example, Samuel told Saul that he would be the first king over Israel before it came to pass (1 Samuel 10:1-9).

How to Use this Weapon: This weapon and gift usually operate automatically in the person who has received it from the Lord or can be activated by request.

The Book of Warfare Weapons
Chapter 26
Word of Wisdom

Most often, it manifests when one is in prayer or worship. The person asks the Holy Spirit, verbally or in tongues, to please let the gift manifest to glorify Jesus Christ, and then by the power of God, it does. When in use, God is revealing to you His mind by the power of the Holy Spirit. You simply declare by faith whatever the Holy Spirit has revealed to you to say.

Secrets of this: In the spirit realm, this weapon (and spiritual gift) is like a top-secret security clearance that gives you access to classified information about future events before they come to pass. This access is hidden from human intellect, reasoning, or wisdom. This weapon (and gift) is 100% accurate and precise. It is not guessing, nor does it rely on human senses (sight, touch, taste, smell, or hearing).

Weapon's Source of Power: The power energizing the weapon and gift of the Word of Wisdom comes from the Holy Spirit.

Faith Heroes Using this Weapon: Elijah (1 Kings 17:1); Elisha (2 Kings 7:1); Prophet Samuel (1 Samuel 10:1-9); Prophetess Deborah (Judges 4:4-24); Prophetess Huldah (2 Kings 22:8-20); and many others.

PICK YOUR CHALLENGE: For a more immersive experience pick your challenge below and complete it according to the instructions listed. For the best experience and maximum impact complete all activities, exercises, and challenges.

Your Challenge: Find ten situations within the Bible where a Word of Wisdom secured victory.

For A Great Challenge: Complete activities in Chapter #26 of *The Book of Warfare Weapons–Workbook*.

Chapter 26
Word of Wisdom

For A Group Challenge: Complete the Group Challenge of Chapter #26 of *The Book of Warfare Weapons–Workbook.*

For A Great Online Challenge: Complete the online activities and challenges in Chapter #26 of *The Book of Warfare Weapons–Outstanding Warrior Challenge (TBOWW-OWC) at* www.tbowowc.com.

Prayer of Activation: Heavenly Father, I pray that You allow this gift to operate in me. Allow me to receive secrets of future events and things of the spirit as You would reveal them. Please help me yield to You, Holy Spirit, and have the faith to operate in it. When You reveal something to me concerning the future, help me to record and track it diligently. I thank You by faith that I have received the spiritual gift of the Word of Wisdom. Thank You, Father, for giving me full access to it by Grace and through the Holy Spirit. In the Name of Jesus Christ, I pray. Amen.

The Book of Warfare Weapons
Chapter 27
Word of Knowledge

Primary Purpose: Reveals information about the past and present
Effective Use: Many enemies
Strength: Very strong

Scriptures:
"For to one is given by the Spirit the word of wisdom; to another the word of knowledge by the same Spirit" (1 Corinthians 12:8).

"For this cause we also, since the day we heard it, do not cease to pray for you, and to desire that ye might be filled with the knowledge of his will in all wisdom and spiritual understanding" (Colossians 1:9).

The Attack: Questions and secrets from your past, or your family's past, rob you of enjoying your present and having a fulfilling future. Vital information that can impact your life today in a significant way is being withheld from you. You need to know something, but forces are working to keep it from you. As a result of what you don't know, you are oppressed, restrained, blocked, hindered, worried, passed over, ostracized, antagonized, and often overlooked.

Weapon of Choice: Word of Knowledge.

Defensively: This powerful weapon is effective against many enemies, but especially against oppression, ignorance, deceit, worry, fears, presumption, defeat, failure, demotion, shame, lies, traps, snares, schemes, and plans of the enemy.

Offensively: This weapon is excellent for bringing confidence, victory, restoration, vindication, protection, revelation, and illumination.

Important Notes for this Weapon: God allows you to know secrets concerning the past and the present with this weapon and spiritual gift. God allows this access for His Glory and to fulfill His purpose. A perfect example of this is Nathan, the prophet confronting King David after David had just sinned – he'd had Uriah killed and had taken Uriah's wife. No one else knew what David had done because he hid it. But Nathan walked in and said, "You are the man (*who did it*)!"

The Book of Warfare Weapons
Chapter 27
Word of Knowledge

He called David out with 100% precision, accuracy, and truth. He did it because he had the weapon (and spiritual gift) of the Word of Knowledge.

How to Use this Weapon: This weapon (gift) operates in the person who has received it from the Lord. Most often, it manifests when one is in prayer or worship. The person asks the Holy Spirit, verbally or in tongues, to please let the gift manifest so praise will come to the Name of Jesus Christ. You believe by faith, and then offer praises and thanksgiving to God until it manifests within you by the Holy Spirit. When in use, God is revealing to you His mind by the power of the Holy Spirit. You simply declare by faith whatever the Holy Spirit has revealed to you to say.

Secrets of this Weapon: In the spirit realm, this weapon (gift) is like a top-secret security clearance that affords you access to hidden things of the past or unknown things occurring at present. This access is hidden from human intellect, reasoning, or wisdom. This weapon (gift) is 100% accurate and precise. It is not guessing, nor does it rely on the human senses (sight, touch, taste, smell, or hearing). It helps to resolve all doubts and to convince a person that Jesus Christ is Lord.

Weapon's Source of Power: The power energizing the weapon (gift) of the Word of Knowledge comes from the Holy Spirit.

Faith Heroes Using this Weapon: Prophetess Ana (Luke 2:36-39); Prophet Nathan (2 Samuel 12:1-12); sons of the prophets (2 Kings 2:5); Elisha (2 Kings 5:26); and many others.

PICK YOUR CHALLENGE: For a more immersive experience pick your challenge below and complete it according to the instructions listed. For the best experience and maximum impact complete all activities, exercises, and challenges.

The Book of Warfare Weapons
Chapter 27
Word of Knowledge

Your Challenge: Have you experienced a Word of Knowledge? How did it impact your life?

For A Great Challenge: Complete activities in Chapter #27 of *The Book of Warfare Weapons–Workbook.*

For A Group Challenge: Complete the Group Challenge of Chapter #27 of *The Book of Warfare Weapons–Workbook.*

For A Great Online Challenge: Complete the online activities and challenges in Chapter #27 of *The Book of Warfare Weapons–Outstanding Warrior Challenge (TBOWW-OWC) online challenge at* www.tbowowc.com.

Prayer of Activation: Heavenly Father, in the mighty Name of Jesus, I thank You so much for making available to me the spiritual gift of Word of Knowledge, wherewith I will be able to understand facts and information of both the past and the present that comes separate from a human understanding of the five human senses. Thank You that when Your Holy Spirit reveals this information to me, it is one hundred percent accurate, precise, and true. I believe by faith that the Holy Spirit desires to share information that will cause me to benefit and have an advantage in this life. Therefore, I yield myself completely to receive this gift. I exercise my faith in the Grace of our Lord Jesus Christ, believing that as I ask for this gift of the Word of Knowledge, it shall operate in my life to fulfill the good purpose of God. I thank You, Father, that it will work even now through the Holy Spirit. I thank you that it shall increase to bring glory and honor to your name. In the Name of Jesus Christ, I pray. Amen.

The Book of Warfare Weapons
Chapter 28
Working of Miracles
Primary Purpose: Gift to release miracles
Effective Use: All enemies
Strength: Unlimited

Scriptures:

"To another the working of miracles; to another prophecy; to another discerning of spirits; to another divers kinds of tongues; to another the interpretation of tongues" (1 Corinthians 12:10). "God also bearing them witness, both with signs and wonders, and with divers miracles, and gifts of the Holy Ghost, according to his own will" (Hebrews 2:4).

The Attack: You have seen, heard, or experienced something devastating. All hope from a natural standpoint seems lost. Defeat appears to be imminent. You may find yourself crying, sobbing, telling yourself that it "can't be true," and hoping that a mistake was made. You feel bad, sick, numb, helpless, worried, regretful, angry, sad, hurt, cheated, discouraged, and scared.

Weapon of Choice: Working of Miracles.

Defensively: This magnificent weapon is excellent in defeating all the powers of darkness and reversing all conditions of defeat to turn them into your victory.

Offensively: This weapon (spiritual gift) is impressive, for it enables one to experience a measure of God's creative "worlds-framing-power" (Hebrews 11:3) that flows through an individual by their faith. The weapon will allow them to flow in a level of victory whereby "nothing is impossible to him that believes" (Mark 9:23).

Important Notes for this Weapon: The primary use of this weapon and spiritual gift is to release miracles. A miracle is required when there is a challenge or problem that is beyond human ability to solve. This weapon (gift) has the power to supersede the laws of nature. An example of this weapon in action was Elisha parting the River Jordan and shutting the heavens for seven years. God used him to work great, mighty miracles.

The Book of Warfare Weapons
Chapter 28
Working of Miracles

How to Use this Weapon: You can ask God for it. Fasting and prayer help to cultivate this weapon and gift within you. You must then rely entirely on the Holy Spirit to empower you in it and allow Him to teach you how to use it. Once you have it, most often, it requires that you are full of the Word of God. Then as the Word of God is in you, the Word will come alive and flow out of you anytime a miracle is needed. Note: This weapon (gift) comes in different levels, measures, and strengths.

Secrets of this Weapon: In the spirit realm, it is like you have received special authority and power from God to suspend the laws of nature temporarily to secure a victory. All manifestations of this gift are, according to the Lord's Will.

Weapon's Source of Power: The power energizing the weapon (gift) of Working of Miracles comes from the Holy Spirit.

Faith Heroes Using this Weapon: Moses (Exodus 7:12); Elisha (2 Kings 2:8); Jacob (Genesis 30:39); Elijah (2 Kings 1:10); and many more.

PICK YOUR CHALLENGE: For a more immersive experience pick your challenge below and complete it according to the instructions listed.
For the best experience and maximum impact complete all activities, exercises, and challenges.

Your Challenge: When are miracles most likely to occur? Is there anything a person can do to increase their chances of experiencing one?

For A Great Challenge: Complete activities in Chapter #28 of *The Book of Warfare Weapons–Workbook.*

The Book of Warfare Weapons
Chapter 28
Working of Miracles

For A Great Online Challenge: Complete the online activities and challenges in Chapter #28 of *The Book of Warfare Weapons—Outstanding Warrior Challenge (TBOWW-OWC) challenge at* <u>*www.tbowowc.com*</u>.

Prayer of Activation: Heavenly Father, I thank You for giving me access to all the Grace of Jesus Christ. From Your Grace comes the Gift of the Working of Miracles. This gift allows Your strength, power, and might to flow through a human vessel to further Your agenda on earth. And so, God, as a candidate whose name is written in Your Lamb's Book of Life, I pray that You allow this grace to operate in my life to help further Your Will. I give You thanks and praise that the Working of Miracles is a part of our spiritual heritage in Jesus Christ. I release my faith to receive miracles, believe in miracles, and operate in miracles by the Holy Spirit. I believe that honor and glory will come to the Name of Jesus Christ as miracles begin to manifest. I give You thanks, Father. In the Name of Jesus Christ, I pray. Amen.

The Book of Warfare Weapons
Chapter 29
Gifts of Healing
Primary Purpose: Gifts of healing
Effective Use: Sickness and diseases
Strength: Extremely strong

Scriptures:
"To another faith by the same Spirit; to another the gifts of healing by the same Spirit" (1 Corinthians 12:9). "Have all the gifts of healing? do all speak with tongues? do all interpret?" (1 Corinthians 12:30).

The Attack: Pain has racked your body or the body of a loved one. Sickness, diseases, or injuries may have weakened your body to the point that it no longer functions the way it once did. You may also notice deformity, swelling, pain, discoloration, sores, discomfort, weakness, odors, discharge, bleeding, and changes in vital signs. You may have sought medical attention, but fear still grips you. The enemy may also tell you that you are going to die or that you have to die. But what does God have to say about the matter?

Weapon of Choice: Gifts of Healing.

Defensively: This powerful weapon is also a spiritual gift. This weapon is effective against all sicknesses, ailments, deformities, injuries, abnormalities, and diseases.

Offensively: This gift is awesome for bringing magnificent glory to God. It proves the redemptive work of Jesus Christ. It is also effective for convincing many of salvation.

Important Notes for this Weapon: The primary purpose of this weapon is to destroy sicknesses and diseases. The weapon accelerates the healing process and restores health and wholeness to the body. There are different degrees of power, measures of anointing, and levels of authority when exercising Gifts of Healing.

How to Use this Weapon: You find someone who is sick. You anoint them with oil, or lay hands on them, or pray over them the prayer of faith, and believe that God will work a miracle, and then the miracle manifests.

The Book of Warfare Weapons
Chapter 29
Gifts of Healing

Secrets of this Weapon: In the spirit realm, this weapon (gift) is like the ultimate restoration center. It can instantly restore a person to perfect health and wholeness in the Name of Jesus Christ.

Weapon's Source of Power: The power energizing the weapon (gift) of Healing comes from the Holy Spirit.

Faith Heroes Using this Weapon: Elisha (2 Kings 5:1-19); Peter and John (Acts 3); Peter (Acts 5:15); Paul (Acts 19:12); and many others.

PICK YOUR CHALLENGE: For a more immersive experience pick your challenge below and complete it according to the instructions listed.
For the best experience and maximum impact complete all activities, exercises, and challenges.

Your Challenge: Is it possible to receive the Gifts of Healing from a prayer of faith? What does the Bible say is necessary to flow in the Gifts of Healing? Are you willing to lay hands on the sick so they may be healed?

For A Great Challenge: Complete activities in Chapter #29 of *The Book of Warfare Weapons–Workbook.*

For A Group Challenge: Complete the Group Challenge of Chapter #29 of *The Book of Warfare Weapons–Workbook.*

For A Great Online Challenge: Complete the online activities and challenges in Chapter #29 of *The Book of Warfare Weapons–Outstanding Warrior Challenge (TBOWW-OWC) online challenge* at _www.tbowowc.com_.

The Book of Warfare Weapons
Chapter 29
Gifts of Healing

Prayer of Activation: Father, I give You thanks and praise that Jesus Christ has come to destroy the works of the devil. He went about doing good, healing all who were sick and afflicted of the enemy, for You were with Him. I thank You, Father, that healing is the children's bread, and that You have made this gift available to us through Your finished work on the cross. Your Word declares that You were wounded for our transgressions, bruised for our iniquities, the chastisement of our peace was upon You, and by Your stripes, we are healed (Isaiah 53:5). I claim healing virtue for my body and declare in Jesus Name that I am healed. Father, I pray that through Your Grace, You will allow Your Gifts of Healing to be made manifest through me. I pray that whomsoever I lay my hands upon who is sick, they will be healed, rescued, and set free by the Holy Spirit. I believe this gift is given to me by faith, and I claim it now. May it manifest gloriously to bring praise and honor to You. I thank You for it, Father. In the Name of Jesus Christ, I pray. Amen.

The Book of Warfare Weapons
Chapter 30
Gift of Faith
Primary Purpose: Gift to release miracles
Effective Use: All enemies
Strength: Unlimited

Scriptures:
"To another faith by the same Spirit; to another the gifts of healing by the same Spirit" (1 Corinthians 12:9).
"And though I have the gift of prophecy, and understand all mysteries, and all knowledge; and though I have all faith, so that I could remove mountains, and have not charity, I am nothing" (1 Corinthians 13:2).

The Attack: Nothing comes easy. It is like you have to fight for every single thing that you receive in life. It is like the enemy is fighting only you. You face opposition everywhere you turn. You expect negative things and may even say words like: "here we go again;" "I knew something bad was going to happen;" or "Why do bad things always happen to me?" As a result, you often feel doubtful, discouraged, negative, bullied, angry, victimized, cheated, lonely, forgotten, or misunderstood.

Weapon of Choice: Gift of Faith.

Defensively: This magnificent weapon is also a spiritual gift. It is highly effective for overcoming all works of the devil. It can change any situation concerning you in Heaven and on earth.

Offensively: This beautiful weapon greatly pleases God. It ushers in an abundance of miracles, signs, and wonders. It is also effective in helping you to change levels in the spirit realm.

Important Notes for this Weapon: This is a weapon (gift) that makes all things possible. It's the weapon and spiritual gift that causes God to move on your behalf. The weapon (gift) has the power to enable you to operate in the "God-kind" of faith. The manifestation is Elijah –how he did such mighty works and miracles, even calling down fire from Heaven and multiplying a meal for three and a half years. Even more incredible – he went to Heaven in a fiery chariot because he dared to believe.

The Book of Warfare Weapons
Chapter 30
Gift of Faith

How to Use this Weapon: This weapon (gift) makes the Word of God come alive within you. The power manifests when the believer exercises his faith to believe God for something. The Holy Spirit dwelling within the believer gives him an extra measure of faith. He can believe for anything. And according to his faith, it shall be done unto him.

Secrets of this Weapon: In the spirit realm, it is like a person has received a special promotion and has become an ambassador to the king. From that highly exalted position of power and authority, whatever they declare or decree in business for King Jesus is an official and legal action of the Kingdom. All of Heaven is there to see to it that it is fulfilled because the King's royal seal is attached to it. The royal seal is the Name of Jesus Christ.

Weapon's Source of Power: The power energizing this weapon- Gift of Faith comes from the Holy Spirit.

Faith Heroes Using this Weapon: Mary (Luke 1:38); Abraham (Romans 4:20-21); Sarah (Hebrews 11:11); Hannah (1 Samuel 1:17-20); Joshua (Joshua 10:13); Gideon (Judges 7); and many others.

PICK YOUR CHALLENGE: For a more immersive experience pick your challenge below and complete it according to the instructions listed.
For the best experience and maximum impact complete all activities, exercises, and challenges.

Your Challenge: The challenge is to name three people who had the Gift of Faith and compare and contrast your life with theirs. Also, ask God to give you the Gift of Faith.

For A Great Challenge: Complete activities in Chapter #30 of *The Book of Warfare Weapons–Workbook.*

The Book of Warfare Weapons
Chapter 30
Gift of Faith

For A Group Challenge: Complete the Group Challenge of Chapter #30 of *The Book of Warfare Weapons–Workbook.*

For A Great Online Challenge: Complete the online activities and challenges in Chapter #30 of *The Book of Warfare Weapons–Outstanding Warrior Challenge (TBOWW-OWC) online challenge at* <u>www.tbowowc.com</u>.

Prayer of Activation: Father, I thank You so much for giving us the spiritual Gift of Faith, wherein You will move on behalf of the person who will release their faith to You. I pray, Father, that You give me this Gift of Faith. Remove all doubt, fear, and unbelief from me. Remove anything that would try to hinder me from walking in the fullness of Your will. I believe by faith that Your faith lives within my heart. Living Jesus, live in me, walk through me, and let the power of Your Holy Spirit be fulfilled in me. Let the Gift of Faith manifest in my life so that honor and glory may come to Your name. I believe that I have received it through the Holy Spirit. I thank You, Father. In the Name of Jesus Christ, I pray. Amen.

The Book of Warfare Weapons
Chapter 31
Divine Dreams
Primary Purpose: Prophetic messages while asleep
Effective Use: Many enemies, especially hopelessness
Strength: Strong

Scriptures:
"And it shall come to pass in the last days, saith God, I will pour out of my Spirit upon all flesh: and your sons and your daughters shall prophesy, and your young men shall see visions, and your old men shall dream dreams" (Acts 2:17). "And it shall come to pass afterward, that I will pour out my spirit upon all flesh; and your sons and your daughters shall prophesy, your old men shall dream dreams, your young men shall see visions" (Joel 2:28).

The Attack: You keep having vivid dreams. You don't know if they are from God, your spirit, or the devil. God has used dreams to help many people in the Bible. The devil can also infiltrate one's dreams at certain times when one's prayer life is weak. Evidence of the enemy attacking through your dreams are times when you experience nightmares, night terrors, wet dreams, spiritual oppressions, spiritual transgressions, and lustful pleasures of the soul called "night fantasies." If the enemy has infiltrated a dream, the person may wake up with fear, anger, bitterness, doubts, thoughts of transgressions, or ideas for numerous acts of sin.

Weapon of Choice: Divine Dreams.

Defensively: This potent weapon is effective against confusion, ignorance, deceit, worry, anxiety, defeat, plans, schemes, plots, and or strategies of the enemy. The weapon is especially effective against hopelessness.

Offensively: This unique weapon is also effective in receiving specific revelation, illumination, knowledge, wisdom, counsel, and instruction from the Lord.

Important Notes for this Weapon: The primary purpose of this gift is to release prophetic messages while one is asleep. A Divine Dream is the activity of the soul communicating with the Spirit of God, or with the human spirit, or with a harassing, unclean spirit while in a suspended state (the latter is what causes nightmares and night terrors). God can give Divine Dreams to the soul, and when He does, they are usually prophetic messages to warn the person to avoid a disaster or prepare to receive a blessing. The meaning of all dreams must be accurately interpreted. Your human speech is the language of your body. Speaking in Tongues is the language of the Spirit. Dreams are the language of the soul.

Note: Divine Dreams are gifts from God, but because few leaders in the church know how to operate in them, interpret them, or discern between them, most churches do not accept or allow Divine Dreams to have a place in church services. This is wrong because none of God's gifts should be refused. Instead, the church should ask God for the wisdom and grace to properly address them. All things in the church must be done in decency, in order, and for the ultimate purpose of bringing glory to God.

How to Use this Weapon: Ask God to give it to you, then receive it by faith. A Divine Dream will usually come at night, the way a regular dream does. When it comes, it will be so vivid and detailed that it would appear as if you were living through the experience. It will seem so real and in living color that you will only know that it was a dream when you open your eyes to find yourself lying in your bed. The moment you wake out of the dream, you should quickly write the dream in your journal before your memory fades. Then pray to God for the interpretation or seek a true Christian who has the Gift of Interpretation to reveal to you, its meaning.

Secrets of this Weapon: With Divine Dreams, God bypasses the human intellect and the human spirit and communicates directly with the soul. It is a remarkable way to receive emotional healing and deliverance.

Weapon's Source of Power: The source of power energizing Divine Dreams comes from God.

The Book of Warfare Weapons
Chapter 31
Divine Dreams

Faith Heroes Using this Weapon: Jacob (Genesis 28:10-22); Joseph (Genesis 37:5-10); Daniel (7:1); Joel's prophecy (Joel 2:28 and Acts 2:17); Joseph, Mary's husband (Matthew 1:20 and 2:13); King Solomon (1 Kings 3:5 and 1 Kings 9:2); and many more.

PICK YOUR CHALLENGE: For a more immersive experience pick your challenge below and complete it according to the instructions listed.
For the best experience and maximum impact complete all activities, exercises, and challenges.

Your Challenge: Ask God to give you divine dreams. Start keeping a journal to track your divine dreams.

For A Great Challenge: Complete activities in Chapter #31 of *The Book of Warfare Weapons–Workbook.*

For A Group Challenge: Complete the Group Challenge of Chapter #31 of *The Book of Warfare Weapons–Workbook.*

For A Great Online Challenge: Complete the online activities and challenges in Chapter #31 of *The Book of Warfare Weapons–Outstanding Warrior Challenge (TBOWW-OWC) online challenge at* www.tbowowc.com.

The Book of Warfare Weapons
Chapter 31
Divine Dreams

Prayer of Activation: Father, in the mighty Name of Jesus, I pray that You purify my dreams. I pray that You will cover my heart, mind, soul, and spirit when I am asleep. I pray that you will inspire all the dreams that come to me. Allow my mind and thoughts to stay on You, for You said You would keep me in perfect peace if my mind stayed on You. Help me to grow in Your Grace, oh God, and may You allow the Divine Dreams that You send me to bring forth messages with clarity. Help me know the difference between the Divine Dreams sent by You and the counterfeit ones the enemy tries to send to deceive me. May Your Holy Fire burn up and destroy all lies, deceits, and deceptions of the enemy. May truth and light be revealed. May You speak to me by Divine Dreams, solving the problems in my life and revealing what is to come through the Holy Spirit. Allow me to interpret each Divine Dream correctly so that their content may guide me to live according to Your Word and perfect will. I believe that it is so. I thank You, Father. In the Name of Jesus Christ, I pray. Amen.

The Book of Warfare Weapons
Chapter 32
Interpretation of Dreams
Primary Purpose: Interpret prophetic messages
Effective Use: Many enemies; especially ignorance
Strength: Strong

Scriptures:
"Then was the secret revealed unto Daniel in a night vision. Then Daniel blessed the God of Heaven" (Daniel 2:19).

"How is it then, brethren? when ye come together, every one of you hath a psalm, hath a doctrine, hath a tongue, hath a revelation, hath an interpretation. Let all things be done unto edifying" (1 Corinthians 14:26).

The Attack: You know that dreams are important, but you don't know what they mean. Sometimes dreams may give you specific answers to life situations, but you forget them as soon as you wake up. You don't know the meaning of your dreams, and you don't know an actual Christian with the gift of Interpretation of Dreams; therefore, worries, doubts, anxiety, fretting, confusion, or thoughts of presumption may then come to your mind.

Weapon of Choice: Interpretation of Dreams.

Defensively: This potent weapon is also a spiritual gift. This weapon is effective against defeat, deception, pride, fear, worry, anxiety, ignorance, snares, traps, schemes, plots, or plans of the enemy.

Offensively: This blessed weapon (gift) is also effective in revealing the mind of God, explicitly concerning a situation. It helps to bring peace, joy, confidence, boldness, encouragement, direction, illumination, and revelation.

Important Notes for this Weapon: This weapon's primary purpose is to interpret prophetic messages contained within dreams and explain their meaning. A person has dreamed a dream but does not know the meaning of it. The enemy wants you to transgress God's Word by turning to tarot card readers, psychics, palm readers, crystal ball gazers, and workers of darkness to receive an answer to your dreams.

94

The Book of Warfare Weapons
Chapter 32
Interpretation of Dreams

Please don't do it, for agents of darkness can't comprehend or interpret messages of light! Additionally, turning to workers of darkness or dark powers will release demons to harass your life. If you need an answer to your dreams, turn to Jesus Christ. God can and will give you a sure answer, and it will be pure truth (Daniel 2:27-28).

How to Use this Weapon: This gift operates automatically by faith. You have a dream, or someone tells you a dream that needs interpreting. You pray and ask God to tell you the meaning of the dream. You then follow the leading of the Holy Spirit and interpret it as He reveals it to you. Say it just as He gives it to you. Do not add to it or take away from it, for all alterations from what is given will taint the message of its accuracy and precision.

Secrets of this Weapon: This weapon (spiritual gift) enables a person to explain the meaning of dreams by the power of God.

Weapon's Source of Power: The power energizing the weapon (gift) of Interpretation of Dreams comes from the Holy Spirit.

Faith Heroes Using this Weapon: Daniel (Daniel 2:36); Joseph (Genesis 41); an unnamed fellow (Judges 7:13-15); and many others.

PICK YOUR CHALLENGE: For a more immersive experience pick your challenge below and complete it according to the instructions listed.
For the best experience and maximum impact complete all activities, exercises, and challenges.

Your Challenge: How many people do you know can interpret dreams? First, find twelve people in the Bible who could interpret dreams. Then, ask God to give you the Gift of Interpretation of Dreams.

The Book of Warfare Weapons
Chapter 32
Interpretation of Dreams

For A Great Challenge: Complete activities in Chapter #32 of *The Book of Warfare Weapons–Workbook*.

For A Group Challenge: Complete the Group Challenge of Chapter #32 of *The Book of Warfare Weapons–Workbook*.

For A Great Online Challenge: Complete the online activities and challenges in Chapter #32 of *The Book of Warfare Weapons–Outstanding Warrior Challenge (TBOWW-OWC) online challenge at* www.tbowowc.com.

Prayer of Activation: Father, I thank You so much that no secret or mystery is hidden from Your sight, and You desire to reveal hidden mysteries to those who will seek unto You. Even as You give all humans dreams, the enemy will sometimes try to come in and bring counterfeit dreams. I pray that You will help me discern what is of You and reject what is not of You by Your Holy Spirit. Help me to bind them in the earth and to cancel them out. But I pray that for all the Divine Dreams You *do* send, You'll allow this gift of Interpretation of Dreams to come forth, either to myself or others.

I pray that the meaning of my dreams will always be made apparent to reveal the truths You would have me know. For your glory, let Your revelation come forth. Father, let this gift of Interpretation of Dreams manifest so that I may know, understand, and walk in the fullness of it through the Holy Spirit. In the Name of Jesus Christ, I pray. Amen.

The Book of Warfare Weapons
Chapter 33
Visions

Primary Purpose: Seeing in the spirit realm
Effective Use: All enemies
Strength: Extremely strong

Scriptures: "As for these four children, God gave them knowledge and skill in all learning and wisdom: and Daniel had understanding in all visions and dreams" (Daniel 1:17). "And it shall come to pass afterward, that I will pour out my spirit upon all flesh; and your sons and your daughters shall prophesy, your old men shall dream dreams, your young men shall see visions" (Joel 2:28).

The Attack: A vision is a direct message from God, given visually and audibly. God chooses when He sends it. It can be before, during, after, or separate from a spiritual attack. It can happen at any time.

Weapon of Choice: Visions.

Defensively: This mighty weapon is effective against evil powers, evil workers, and evil plans of darkness and wickedness.

Offensively: This weapon brings light, illumination, revelation, direction, faith, peace, strength, faith, guidance, instruction, knowledge, understanding, wisdom, and victory (Acts 26:19).

Important Notes for this Weapon: This weapon's primary use is the ability to see in the spirit realm when enabled to do so by God. The perfect example is the prophet Ezekiel. He saw astonishing visions, great signs, and mighty wonders – some of which are still a mystery to Bible scholars even today. He was one of the only prophets who saw them, especially those involving things hard to understand like: holy living creatures, a wheel in a wheel, and things of the Glory of God that cannot be easily explained.

How to Use this Weapon: This is a weapon and spiritual gift given and controlled entirely by God. As the believer spends more time in consecration, worship, prayer, and the Word of God, the visions will occur more frequently and with greater depth of perception.

The Book of Warfare Weapons
Chapter 33
Visions

Secrets of this Weapon: In the spirit realm, it is as if God simply rolls back the curtain between temporal and eternal, time and space, to allow one to see clearly in the spirit realm as it pleases Him.

Weapon's Source of Power: The power energizing the weapon of Visions comes from the Holy Spirit.

Faith Heroes Using this Weapon: Ezekiel (Ezekiel 1:1); Isaiah (Isaiah 1:1); Jeremiah (Jeremiah 24:1); John (Revelation 1:1-10); and many others.

PICK YOUR CHALLENGE: For a more immersive experience pick your challenge below and complete it according to the instructions listed.
For the best experience and maximum impact complete all activities, exercises, and challenges.

Your Challenge: In your opinion, how would your life be any different if you received a vision from God? What changes do you think you would make, if any?

For A Great Challenge: Complete activities in Chapter #33 of *The Book of Warfare Weapons–Workbook.*

For A Group Challenge: Complete the Group Challenge of Chapter #33 of *The Book of Warfare Weapons–Workbook.*

For A Great Online Challenge: Complete the online activities and challenges in Chapter #33 of *The Book of Warfare Weapons–Outstanding Warrior Challenge (TBOWW-OWC) online challenge at* www.tbowowc.com.

The Book of Warfare Weapons
Chapter 33
Visions

Prayer of Activation: Heavenly Righteous Father, in the mighty Name of Jesus, I give You thanks and praise for using the spiritual gift of Visions as a method of revealing Your will to me. I ask You, Father, to give me the grace to see heavenly visions that would help me to fulfill Your divine will for my life. I believe that You hear me, and I have that I ask of You through the Holy Spirit. I thank You for it, Father. In the Name of Jesus Christ, I pray. Amen.

The Book of Warfare Weapons
Chapter 34
Signs

Primary Purpose: Hidden mysteries observed
Effective Use: Many enemies, especially doubt
Strength: Divine class

Scriptures:

"And there shall be signs in the sun, and in the moon, and in the stars; and upon the earth distress of nations, with perplexity; the sea and the waves roaring" (Luke 21:25). "God also bearing them witness, both with signs and wonders, and with divers miracles, and gifts of the Holy Ghost, according to his own will" (Hebrews 2:4).

The Attack: A sign is a direct form of evidence from God, usually accompanying the gift of Miracles, gifts of Healings, and the gift of Faith. God chooses when He sends it. It most often appears during an attack or soon after to reverse the attack's power and results. It usually brings great embarrassment to the enemy and great Glory to God.

Weapon of Choice: Signs.

Defensively: This excellent and living weapon is part of the divine class of weapons and can defeat or change anything in creation. It is especially effective against lies, heresies, confusion, unbelief, and deception.

Offensively: This weapon helps to convince a person with 100% certainty that the gospel of Jesus Christ is true, for God confirms the gospel by sending signs from Heaven so that men may be saved. It is essential for an ever-increasing, highly fruitful, powerful, and long-sustaining ministry (Acts 2:22).

Important Notes for this Weapon: This weapon causes supernatural occurrences to manifest following revelation or prophecy. The primary use of signs is to confirm the Word of God. Therefore, the sign is tangible evidence related to the divine work of God on earth.

How to Use this Weapon: Ask God to give it to you and to flow through you so that Jesus Christ may receive glory.

The Book of Warfare Weapons
Chapter 34
Signs

Be faithful in spending time with God in worship, prayer, and studying the Word of God. Look for an opportunity to operate in Signs when preaching the gospel, leading someone to salvation, manifesting deliverance, or administering healings.

Secrets of this Weapon: It is like seeing the creative hand of God (that formed the worlds) move on your behalf to the point of suspending the laws of nature temporarily to give you victory.

Weapon's Source of Power: The source of power energizing this weapon comes from the Gift of God.

Faith Heroes Using this Weapon: Moses (Deuteronomy 43:11); Philip (Acts 6:12-13); Stephen (Acts 6:8); Paul & Barnabas (Acts 14:3); and many more.

PICK YOUR CHALLENGE: For a more immersive experience pick your challenge below and complete it according to the instructions listed. For the best experience and maximum impact complete all activities, exercises, and challenges.

Your Challenge: Find five Signs that occurred in the Bible and seek to understand the circumstances under which they occurred.

For A Great Challenge: Complete activities in Chapter #34 of *The Book of Warfare Weapons–Workbook.*

For A Group Challenge: Complete the Group Challenge of Chapter #34 of *The Book of Warfare Weapons–Workbook.*

For A Great Online Challenge: Complete the online activities and challenges in Chapter #34 of *The Book of Warfare Weapons–Outstanding Warrior Challenge (TBOWW-OWC) online challenge* at www.tbowowc.com.

The Book of Warfare Weapons
Chapter 34
Signs

Prayer of Activation: Heavenly Righteous Father, in the mighty Name of Jesus, I thank You so much that You have given me the gift of Signs. May You use them, Father, to destroy all doubt, and every lie that the enemy will try to bring to cause problems for me. I trust in the more excellent Signs that Jesus performed on the Cross of Calvary. The Sign of being pierced in His side, and there came out blood and water. The Sign of the crown of thorns He wore for me to take away my shame. The Sign that the veil in the temple was rent from top to bottom, so I can have full access to the Holy of Holies presence of God daily. The Sign of Jesus's empty tomb, because He lives, I too shall live with Him forever. Signs help to bring to light hidden mysteries so that we can observe them and understand them. May You continue to reveal the manifestation of their purpose, and may You enable me to fulfill the good pleasure of Your will as I go forth in faith. I believe they shall manifest for Your Glory through the Holy Spirit. I look forward to their appearance. I thank You, Father. In the Name of Jesus Christ, I pray. Amen.

The Book of Warfare Weapons
Chapter 35
Wonders
Primary Purpose: Hidden mysteries in action
Effective Use: Many enemies, especially unbelief
Strength: Divine class

Scriptures:
"And the Lord showed signs and wonders, great and sore, upon Egypt, upon Pharaoh, and upon all his household, before our eyes" (Deuteronomy 6:22). "Through mighty signs and wonders, by the power of the Spirit of God; so that from Jerusalem, and round about unto Illyricum, I have fully preached the gospel of Christ" (Romans 15:19).

The Attack: Occurrences where God moves to suspend the laws of nature to accomplish His Will, apart from the involvement of mankind. God usually sends it to accompany miracles, signs, healings, and the Gift of faith. It most often appears during an attack or soon after to reverse the attack's power and results. It severely embarrasses the enemy and brings tremendous glory to God.

Weapon of Choice: Wonders.

Defensively: This excellent and living weapon is part of the divine class of weapons and can defeat or change anything in creation. It is especially effective against fear, doubt, and unbelief.

Offensively: This weapon allows the believer to exercise the believer's power of redemption, whereas Jesus promised, "Verily, verily, I say unto you, He that believeth on me, the works that I do shall he do also; and greater works than these shall he do; because I go unto my Father" (John 14:12).

Important Notes for this Weapon: This weapon releases God's power, which supersedes all the laws of creation to give a person victory. Moses was one person who experienced numerous Wonders of God. He witnessed the parting of the Red Sea, ten plagues of Egypt, water from a rock, Hell opening for receiving rebels, food from Heaven for 40 years, and many more.

The Book of Warfare Weapons
Chapter 35
Wonders

How to Use this Weapon: This excellent weapon is controlled entirely by God. God will manifest it whenever it is necessary to fulfill His divine Will or help his servants. To operate in it, you must have a very close relationship with God. Make it your goal to become God's very best friend and to have great faith in His Word. Then, when the need arises, God will work wonders on your behalf because He is a "wonders-working-God."

Secrets of this Weapon: In the spirit realm, your close relationship with God gives you access that few others will ever experience. This complete access to God is based on love for God, NOT duty to God. Many people are faithful employees of God, but few choose to be His friend. This level of power is reserved for friends of God alone. The Bible states, that Abraham was a friend of God (James 2:23).

Weapon's Source of Power: The power of wonders comes from the very presence of God (usually His Glory), as administered by the Holy Spirit, in the Name of Jesus Christ.

Faith Heroes Using this Weapon: Moses (Exodus 14 & 33:11); Joshua (10:12-13); Shadrach, Meshach, and Abednego (Daniel 3:19-25); Elijah (2 Kings 2:11); and many more.

PICK YOUR CHALLENGE: For a more immersive experience pick your challenge below and complete it according to the instructions listed. For the best experience and maximum impact complete all activities, exercises, and challenges.

Your Challenge: Find seven Wonders that occurred in the Bible and seek to understand why they occurred.

For A Great Challenge: Complete activities in Chapter #35 of *The Book of Warfare Weapons—Workbook.*

The Book of Warfare Weapons
Chapter 35
Wonders

For A Group Challenge: Complete the Group Challenge of Chapter #35 of *The Book of Warfare Weapons–Workbook*.

For A Great Online Challenge: Complete the online activities and challenges in Chapter #35 of *The Book of Warfare Weapons–Outstanding Warrior Challenge (TBOWW-OWC) online challenge* at _www.tbowowc.com_.

Prayer of Activation: Father, I thank You that because of our exalted and glorified Savior Jesus Christ, I have access to You working Wonders in my life. God, I believe that Wonders are a part of the benefit of salvation. Therefore, I pray that it may be made manifest in whatever area of my life needs Your wonder-working power. Allow it to come forth and set in order everything that is upside down, torn, or broken. May it activate to fix what is missing, destroyed, lacking, barren, and non-producing in my life. Let the Wonders of God manifest the mysteries of salvation and the benefits of grace in my life. I exercise my faith right now to receive whatever wonder-working power of God that You desire to release in my life through the Holy Spirit. I believe and I thank You for it, Father. In the Name of Jesus Christ, I pray. Amen.

The Book of Warfare Weapons
Chapter 36
Anointing with Oil
Primary Purpose: Invoking the Holy Spirit
Effective Use: Fleshly works
Strength: Very strong

Scriptures:
"Thou preparest a table before me in the presence of mine enemies: thou anointest my head with oil; my cup runneth over" (Psalm 23:5).
"Then shalt thou take the anointing oil, and pour it upon his head, and anoint him" (Exodus 29:7).
"My head with oil thou didst not anoint: but this woman hath anointed my feet with ointment" (Luke 7:46).
"And thou shalt make it an oil of holy ointment, an ointment compound after the art of the apothecary: it shall be a holy anointing oil" (Exodus 30:25).

The Attack: You are being oppressed or opposed. The enemy is harassing or oppressing you, your family, or your loved ones. You or a loved one is sick and in need of healing. You need protection, peace, or promotion.

Weapon of Choice: Anointing with Oil.

Defensively: This powerful weapon is effective against all the defeating powers of darkness. It destroys plots, schemes, traps, snares, abuse, attacks, ambush, sabotage, abortions, dangers, thefts, confusion, violence, addictions, bondages, demotions, defeat, shame, and ridicule.

Offensively: This gift brings protection, deliverance, preservation, promotion, and favor. It is also effective for bringing healing from sicknesses and disease (James 5:14).

Important Notes for this Weapon: It has various purposes. It is used for consecration, transferring anointing, and as a point of contact. Its primary purpose is to invoke the Holy Spirit. It's effective against all fleshly works. It's very strong. It is used to bring something to a consecrated position. The manifestation of it is Samuel anointing David with oil, and the challenge is to anoint with oil or get anointed with oil.

It's also exceptional for the transferring of spiritual things; like spiritual authority, wisdom, and spiritual gifts. Do not put it on those who are mad, rebels, evil workers, those who sold themselves to work evil, or demons possessed. Deliverance from demons should be through the power of the Word, not anointing with holy oil (Matthew 8:16). The anointing with oil is reserved for those whom God approves (the redeemed) and those who are sick (James 5:14).

How to Use this Weapon: First, select good quality oil. The oil of choice is usually virgin olive oil or extra virgin olive oil. Then, ask a Christian man or woman full of faith to pray over it to consecrate it unto the Lord. Once the oil is blessed and sanctified, be sure never to use it for everyday purposes like cooking. The holy oil must be set apart from common use and reserved only for spiritual matters. For example, if you want to activate protection, pray and anoint with oil: yourself, your home, your family, and everything you want to be protected. Next, pray and declare the Word of God. Finally, end by giving God thanks and praise in the Name of Jesus Christ.

Secrets of this Weapon: In the spirit realm, this is a spiritual seal and a spiritual mark. It is similar to branding. Those with eyes to see in the spirit can at times see believers who are marked for God. It marks you for the blessings and favor of God while serving notice to the enemy to "keep back" because you belong to God.

Weapon's Source of Power: This amazing weapon is energized by the wisdom of God. It represents the Spirit of God resting upon a person and is used as a point of contact for the holy anointing to rest.

Faith Heroes Using this Weapon: Moses anointed Aaron the High Priest (Exodus 30:30); Samuel anointed David (1 Samuel 16:13); and many others.

The Book of Warfare Weapons
Chapter 36
Anointing with Oil

PICK YOUR CHALLENGE: For a more immersive experience pick your challenge below and complete it according to the instructions listed.
For the best experience and maximum impact complete all activities, exercises, and challenges.

Your Challenge: Ask your pastor to anoint your bottle of oil. Frequently anoint yourself with oil in the Name of Jesus Christ. What changes did you notice after a week?

For A Great Challenge: Complete activities in Chapter #36 of *The Book of Warfare Weapons–Workbook*.

For A Group Challenge: Complete the Group Challenge of Chapter #36 of *The Book of Warfare Weapons–Workbook*.

For A Great Online Challenge: Complete the online activities and challenges in Chapter #36 of *The Book of Warfare Weapons–Outstanding Warrior Challenge (TBOWW-OWC) online challenge at* www.tbowowc.com.

Prayer of Activation: Father, I thank You that You have given me the revelation of anointing with oil that comes through Jesus Christ. Even as I apply this oil by the leading of Your Holy Spirit, may it accomplish the work you desire to achieve. May You use this anointing oil as a spiritual point of contact. Whenever I anoint something with oil, may the power of the Holy Spirit be made manifest on the scene to accomplish Your will, Holy Father. Following Your eternal Word, I now exercise my faith to anoint with oil. Let the Anointing oil be used and set aside for consecrated use through the Holy Spirit. May Your kingdom be advanced as I apply it, in accordance with Your Word. Thank You for it, Father. I believe that I receive it. In the Name of Jesus Christ, I pray. Amen.

The Book of Warfare Weapons
Chapter 37
Laying on of Hands
Primary Purpose: Transferring spiritual things
Effective Use: All enemies
Strength: Very strong

Scriptures:

"Of the doctrine of baptisms, and of laying on of hands, and of resurrection of the dead, and of eternal judgment" (Hebrews 6:2).

"As they ministered to the Lord, and fasted, the Holy Ghost said, Separate me Barnabas and Saul for the work whereunto I have called them. And when they have fasted and prayed, and laid their hands on them, they sent them away" (Acts 13:2-3).

The Attack: You don't have or know your spiritual gift. You feel you can't receive the Holy Spirit Baptism. You have no spiritual power, or your spiritual cup is dry. You need the power of generational curses, addictions, and bondage to be destroyed in your life. You or a loved one is suffering from sickness, infirmity, or disease.

Weapon of Choice: Laying on of Hands.

Defensively: This powerful weapon is effective against oppression, harassment, confusion, division, dangers, attacks, threats, discord, sicknesses, a troubled mind, anxiety, depression, sadness, lies, demotion, shame, bondage, and ridicule.

Offensively: This weapon brings healing, deliverance, restoration, promotion, increase, strength, vindication, an increased measure of spiritual anointing, a greater capacity for faith, the deposit and activation of spiritual gifts, and Baptism in the Holy Spirit (Acts 8:18-19).

Important Notes for this Weapon: It is used to transfer blessings, appoint for leadership, consecrate for service, and as an obedient act to initiate healing. Additional uses are to deposit, release, and activate gifts within an individual. The measure given to the apostles was so powerful that those whom they laid hands upon were instantly filled with the Baptism of the Holy Spirit (Acts 8:18-19).

The Book of Warfare Weapons
Chapter 37
Laying on of Hands

Yet, the Word also cautions all to be careful not to lay hands suddenly on any man (1 Timothy 5:22). Spirits are transferrable. Therefore, make sure you know those who labor among you before you allow any to lay hands on you. Those trustworthy, full of faith, love, humility, and faithful works for Christ, esteem them highly in love (1 Thessalonians 5:12-13) and allow them only to lay hands on you.

How to Use this Weapon: As the Holy Spirit leads or as the situation warrant, begin to pray, asking for the Holy Spirit to take complete control. Then, pray whatever the Lord gives you to pray. You may also Anoint with Oil and then administer the Laying on of Hands (these two weapons are often used together). Pray from your spirit according to the will of God while initiating the Laying on of Hands.

Secrets of this Weapon: In the spirit realm, it is an instantaneous day of promotion for whomsoever has anointed hands laid upon them in faith and prayer. A measure of the faith, power, and anointing that rests upon the believer is instantly transferred to the receiver through the Laying on of Hands; therefore, one should not lay hands frivolously, but with understanding and purposeful intention.

Weapon's Source of Power: The power energizing this weapon comes from the body of Jesus Christ.

Faith Heroes Using this Weapon: Isaac (Genesis 27); Jacob (Genesis 48:8-22); Moses (Numbers 27:23); Paul (2 Timothy 1:6) and many more.

PICK YOUR CHALLENGE: For a more immersive experience pick your challenge below and complete it according to the instructions listed. For the best experience and maximum impact complete all activities, exercises, and challenges.

The Book of Warfare Weapons
Chapter 37
Laying on of Hands

Your Challenge: Ask your pastor or an anointed leader to lay hands on you to impart a blessing to you.

For A Great Challenge: Complete activities in Chapter #37 of *The Book of Warfare Weapons–Workbook.*

For A Group Challenge: Complete the Group Challenge of Chapter #37 of *The Book of Warfare Weapons–Workbook.*

For A Great Online Challenge: Complete the online activities and challenges in Chapter #37 of *The Book of Warfare Weapons–Outstanding Warrior Challenge (TBOWW-OWC) online challenge at* www.tbowowc.com.

Prayer of Activation: Father, I thank You for Jesus, who is our risen and ascended Savior. He is seated at Your right hand. Jesus has given us revelation of exercising power, might, and dominion on earth, even by the simple act of the Laying on of Hands. So I pray, Father, that all the power You have given me through the Holy Spirit will manifest when I lay hands to fulfill Your will. May people be healed, delivered, rescued, and set free. May miracles, Signs, and Wonders manifest. May promotion come forth. May You bring confirmation by imparting spiritual gifts. May every desire of Your heart be fulfilled as Your Holy Spirit directs me with the simple act of the Laying on of Hands. May I succeed in Laying on of Hands as I walk in obedience to Your Holy Spirit and Your Word. I give You thanks and praise, Father, believing that it is so. In the Name of Jesus Christ, I pray. Amen.

The Book of Warfare Weapons
Chapter 38
Fasting
Primary Purpose: Advance power to spirit
Effective Use: All enemies
Strength: Extremely strong

Scriptures:

"That thou appear not unto men to fast, but unto thy Father which is in secret: and thy Father which seeth in secret, shall reward thee openly" (Matthew 6:18).

"And I set my face unto the Lord God, to seek by prayer and supplications, with fasting, and sackcloth, and ashes" (Daniel 9:3).

The Attack: All your plans have ended in disaster. You are under extreme pressure or a spiritual attack. You need help against all forces that are opposing you. All your enemies want to see you fall. Shame and embarrassment are taunting you. Fear is tormenting you. You feel like giving up, walking away, and calling it quits. You feel spiritually numb, tired, weary, weak, or drained. Does Fasting work? Can it help change your situation? Absolutely, yes!!!

Weapon of Choice: Fasting.

Defensively: This mighty weapon is effective against all opposition, oppression, and all powers of the enemy.

Offensively: The exercising of this weapon can help a believer receive from God any gift, fruit, blessing, grace, weapon, deliverance, healing, or victory.

Important Notes for this Weapon: Fasting is a time of consecration wherein a person avoids food as they seek the face of God. People fast for many different reasons. The more common reasons are to chasten one's soul before God, when in mourning, when seeking an answer from God, for healing, deliverance, and strength.

The primary use is to advance the power of faith to the spirit of man while drawing closer to God. This weapon is an exercise of spiritual activity. It strengthens the human spirit while abstaining from foods. Fasting should always accompany studying the Word of God and participating in prayer.

The Book of Warfare Weapons
Chapter 38
Fasting

Prayer is essential to Fasting. A fast without prayer is simply a "no foods diet." It is powerless, fruitless, and a waste of time. But Fasting with prayer is the spiritual catalyst to produce miracles, signs, and wonders.

How to Use this Weapon: Schedule a set time to fast by having a start time and a stop time. During this time, avoid foods. Instead, use the time that you would typically eat to read the Word of God and pray. Abstain from all pleasures, fleshly lusts, and sensual activities, including TV, social media, movies, video games, etc. Instead, use the time to draw closer to God, hear His voice, and yield entirely to Him. Give Him abundant praise during and especially after the fast (with confidence that your prayers have all been answered).

Secrets of this Weapon: In the spirit realm, the oldest and most stubborn of all sins is the sin of pride. All other sins oppose God's laws, precepts, and works, but pride opposes God Himself. Therefore, God is moved to bring low all lifted in pride, but He gives grace to the humble. Fasting is one of the most remarkable ways of humbling the spirit, soul, and body before God. God then lifts and gives grace to all who fast before Him in sincerity.

Weapon's Source of Power: This weapon's energy source comes from the meekness, humility, trust, and obedience of our Savior, Jesus Christ.

Faith Heroes Using this Weapon: *Most importantly Jesus fasted 40 days and nights (Matthew 4:2); Queen Esther (Esther 4:16); Moses (Exodus 34:28); Elijah (1 Kings 19:8); Isaiah (Isaiah 58:6-11); Daniel (Daniel 1:8-16); Prophetess Ana (Luke 2:36-37); disciples of John (Luke 5:33); Jesus says we should all fast after His resurrection (Luke 5:35, also Matthew 17:21); The church, apostles, prophets, and teachers (Acts 13:1-3); and many others.

The Book of Warfare Weapons
Chapter 38
Fasting

PICK YOUR CHALLENGE: For a more immersive experience pick your challenge below and complete it according to the instructions listed. For the best experience and maximum impact complete all the activities, exercises, and challenges.

Your Challenge: Set a time to fast this week.

For A Great Challenge: Complete activities in Chapter #38 of *The Book of Warfare Weapons–Workbook*.

For A Group Challenge: Complete the Group Challenge of Chapter #38 of *The Book of Warfare Weapons–Workbook*.

For A Great Online Challenge: Complete the online activities and challenges in Chapter #38 of *The Book of Warfare Weapons–Outstanding Warrior Challenge (TBOWW-OWC) online challenge at* www.tbowowc.com.

Prayer of Activation: Heavenly Father, in the mighty Name of Jesus, I thank You so much for giving us this spiritual act of obedience called Fasting. I thank You that it allows me to exercise my faith through obedience unto You. By faith, I acknowledge that man does not live by bread alone but by every word that proceeded out of Your mouth. So, when I set aside food and seek Your face through Fasting, may it be acceptable in Your sight. May it be a time that I draw near to You. May it be a time where I receive the strength to hear Your voice more clearly. May it be a time for more of You and less of me. Fulfill Your every desire in my life as a result of this fast. May Your glory be my re-reward and cause victory in my life to break forth speedily, as my health is suddenly renewed (Isaiah 58:8). And even during this time, ignite my life to become a blaze of fire, too hot for the enemy to handle. May the Holy Spirit take complete control of my life. Fulfill Your purpose in my life and change me to become more like Jesus. I thank You that through this fast, I will experience victory in every area of my life. I give You thanks and praise, Father. In the Name of Jesus Christ, I pray. Amen.

The Book of Warfare Weapons
Chapter 39
Water Baptism
Primary Purpose: Divine act, purifies the conscience
Effective Use: Condemnation and shame
Strength: Extremely strong

Scriptures:
"And Jesus, when he was baptized, went up straightway out of the water: and lo, the heavens were opened unto him, and he saw the Spirit of God descending like a dove, and lighting upon him: And lo a voice from heaven, saying, This is my beloved Son, in whom I am well pleased" (Matthew 3:16-17). "And I knew him not: but he that sent me to baptize with water, the same said unto me, Upon whom thou shalt see the Spirit descending, and remaining on him, the same is he which baptizeth with the Holy Ghost" (John 1:33).

The Attack: You are not sure if you are genuinely saved. You want to please God, but your habits are just too strong for you. You have difficulty forgiving yourself for your past mistakes and sins. You want to join a church but don't feel worthy. You battle condemnation, shame, embarrassment, regrets, mocking, or scorning. You are afraid and ashamed to let anyone know you love Jesus, especially those close to you. You never witness or tell anyone else about Jesus.

Weapon of Choice: Water Baptism.

Defensively: The excellent and enduring weapon of Water Baptism is an unveiled mystery of Heaven that reflects the mystery of our resurrection with Jesus Christ. It is effective against all shame, disobedience, rebellion, stubbornness, pride, division, peer pressure, mocking, scorning, ridicule, and condemnation.

Offensively: This gift brings unity, acceptance, joy, peace, strength, refreshing, boldness, meekness, and favor. It purifies the conscience and brings confidence toward God (1 Peter 3:21).

Important Notes for this Weapon: The primary use of this weapon works as a spiritual action that purifies the conscience and destroys guilt.

The Book of Warfare Weapons
Chapter 39
Water Baptism

It is effective against all forms of condemnation. The revelation is Water Baptism reveals a divine mystery of redemption. A perfect example of it is John the Baptist, as he was called by God and went about baptizing in water. The challenge for the individual is to submit to water baptism as an act of obedience to God's divine command (Matthew 28:19). Therefore, every time the enemy tries to bring condemnation from past sins, remembering that you were baptized into Jesus Christ releases fresh power to free your mind and conscience. The Blood of Jesus releases this fresh power.

How to Use this Weapon: Take the new believer to a body of water (or a baptismal pool). Have them confess (before all who are present) that they have repented of their sins, accepted Jesus as their Lord and Savior, and have decided to be a disciple of Jesus Christ. Then say, "On the confession of your faith in Jesus Christ, I baptize you with water unto repentance. "In the Name of the Father, the Son, and the Holy Ghost (Matthew 28:19) and the Name of Jesus Christ (Acts 2:38), Amen." Then, dip the person (fully submerged) under the water. Finally, bring the person up again while instructing the person to give praise to God.

Secrets of this Weapon: In the spirit realm, all who are redeemed and obedient to the Father will yield and submit themselves to Water Baptism as Jesus did. It is a spiritual act, declaring to all in Heaven that the believer has identified with the resurrection of Jesus Christ and is willing to die for his faith. It also speaks to the victory that each believer will experience as they will triumph over death, Hell, and the grave. Also, you are letting Heaven know that you understand the mystery. This spiritual act of Water Baptism is like a club initiation or a secret handshake of membership of the redeemed. You will participate in the first resurrection because you are counted in the group as redeemed of the Lord. Water Baptism is an outward sign that you have reservations to participate in the first resurrection (Revelation 20:5-6).

The Book of Warfare Weapons
Chapter 39
Water Baptism

Weapon's Source of Power: This weapon is energized by the Lordship of Jesus Christ.

Faith Heroes Using this Weapon: *Most importantly, Jesus submitted Himself to baptism (Matthew 3:15); others who performed it included John the Baptist (Luke 3:3); Peter (Acts 10:47-48); Philip (Acts 8:35-40); and Paul (Acts 16:33).

PICK YOUR CHALLENGE: For a more immersive experience pick your challenge below and complete it according to the instructions listed. For the best experience and maximum impact complete all activities, exercises, and challenges.

Your Challenge: Make an appointment to get baptized as soon as possible and encourage others to do it.

For A Great Challenge: Complete activities in Chapter #39 of *The Book of Warfare Weapons–Workbook.*

For A Group Challenge: Complete the Group Challenge of Chapter #39 of *The Book of Warfare Weapons–Workbook.*

For A Great Online Challenge: Complete the online activities and challenges in Chapter #39 of *The Book of Warfare Weapons–Outstanding Warrior Challenge (TBOWW-OWC) online challenge at www.tbowowc.com.*

The Book of Warfare Weapons
Chapter 39
Water Baptism

Prayer of Activation: O Father, I thank You so much for baptizing me into Christ when I accepted salvation. I thank You, Jesus Christ, for baptizing me in the power of the Holy Spirit. I pray, dear God, even as I participate in Water Baptism, that the realities and the revelation of baptism on all three levels will be made manifest continually in my life. As I submit myself in obedience to Water Baptism, may the full strength of the revelation of the life of Christ manifest within me. May the revelation that as He rose from the grave, I too will rise from the grave with power and strength when I receive my glorified body. May this truth manifest with me that Jesus was the first fruit born among many brethren. I will be a second fruit, coming forth in the strength of His resurrection. I thank You for the realities of Water Baptism that took place for my body, my spirit, and my soul. May the Holy Spirit strengthen me to live in such a way that You will receive all the honor and glory from my life. I believe, and I thank You for it, Father. In the Name of Jesus Christ, I pray. Amen.

The Book of Warfare Weapons
Chapter 40
Communion
Primary Purpose: Divine act, brings many blessings
Effective Use: Sickness and disease
Strength: Divine class

Scriptures:

"And he took bread, and gave thanks, and brake it, and gave unto them, saying, *This is my body which is given for you: this do in remembrance of me*" (Luke 22:19). "For I have received of the Lord that which also I delivered unto you, that the Lord Jesus the same night in which he was betrayed took bread: And when he had given thanks, he brake it, and said, Take, eat: this is my body, which is broken for you: this do in remembrance of me" (1 Corinthians 11:23-24).

The Attack: You don't understand why Jesus died for you and don't see the importance of taking Communion. You think it is merely an old tradition passed down through the years, which is not relevant for us today. You don't participate in Communion because you are too busy or don't feel like it.

Weapon of Choice: Communion.

Defensively: This weapon is in the divine class. It was administered to all by the Lord Jesus Christ, and it has power in Heaven and on earth. It is a revealed mystery of redemption and the resurrection. It is effective against all the powers of darkness, especially division, discord, bondage, sickness, and disease.

Offensively: This excellent gift brings us into fellowship with Jesus Christ and allows us to partake of His life. It brings vitality, health, recovery, unity, acceptance, humility, grace, breakthrough, obedience, and deliverance. It also reconfirms the conditions and benefits of our new covenant each time we partake of it.

Important Notes for this Weapon: Communion is a time of fellowship, remembering the price that Jesus paid in giving His life as a ransom for our sins. Communion is also called the Lord's Supper. Communion is a divine act that brings many blessings.

119

The Book of Warfare Weapons
Chapter 40
Communion

Communion is the partaking of the Body (bread) and Blood (grape juice which is new wine; not old wine, which is fermented) of Jesus Christ.

When we eat of the Body (bread) and Blood (wine) of our Lord Jesus Christ, we are receiving the power of His life. When we honor what He has done for us, our faith is renewed, our spirit is strengthened, our soul is justified, and our body is healed.

How to Use this Weapon: Please note that Communion should be administered by ministers of the gospel whenever possible. If there are no ministers available, take your Bible and read 1 Corinthians 11:20-34. Make sure to read the warning and cautions that will come upon all who take Communion unworthily (weakness, sickness, and even death). No sinner should ever partake of Communion, for to do so is eating damnation unto themselves (1 Corinthians 11:29). It is reserved for all who are redeemed. Also, whatever portions of Communion (bread and wine) are hollowed, consecrated, and blessed must be consumed entirely. None of it should be left behind after Communion, and none should be discarded or thrown away. Therefore, it is advisable to prepare small portions (but even the small portions are potent). Follow the guidelines in the Bible by first blessing the bread, then eating it, then blessing the wine, and drinking it. Focus on Jesus, and worship Him with love, honor, and thanksgiving.

Secrets of this Weapon: You are partaking of the life of Jesus Christ each time you participate in Communion.

Weapon's Source of Power: This weapon is energized by the love, body, blood, and life of Jesus Christ.

Faith Heroes Using this Weapon: Jesus at the Last Supper (Matthew 26; Mark 14; Luke 22; John 13); and all saints everywhere.

PICK YOUR CHALLENGE: For a more immersive experience pick your challenge below and complete it according to the instructions listed.

The Book of Warfare Weapons
Chapter 40
Communion

For the best experience and maximum impact complete all activities, exercises, and challenges.

Your Challenge: Make sure to take Communion the next time your church offers it.

For A Great Challenge: Complete activities in Chapter #40 of *The Book of Warfare Weapons–Workbook*.

For A Group Challenge: Complete the Group Challenge of Chapter #40 of *The Book of Warfare Weapons–Workbook*.

For A Great Online Challenge: Complete the online activities and challenges in Chapter #40 of *The Book of Warfare Weapons–Outstanding Warrior Challenge (TBOWW-OWC)* at <u>www.tbowowc.com</u>.

Prayer of Activation: Father, I thank You for giving us the spiritual blessing of Communion. As often as we do it, we do it in remembrance of our Lord and Savior, Jesus Christ. Thank You that He gave His life for our ransom. His body was broken, and His Blood was shed that we may have life and have it more abundantly, to the full and running over. Now, God, I pray in the Name of Jesus Christ that the full strength of Communion will manifest in my life. May all sicknesses, pain, disease, or ailments that come to attack my health be destroyed by the power of the body of Jesus Christ when I take Communion. I believe that the life of Jesus Christ energizes my body each time I partake in Communion. The life of Christ comes in me, as it is written, "I am crucified with Christ, nevertheless I live, yet not I, but Christ liveth in me; and the life which I now live in the flesh I live by faith in the Son of God, who loved me, gave Himself for me"(Galatians 2:20). I thank You that as often as I participate in Communion, I have fellowship with You, Father, Jesus Christ, and the Holy Spirit. May the full revelation that is hidden in this spiritual act manifest within me. May You draw me closer to Your presence. May I live out the fullness of the God-kind of life on the earth through the Holy Spirit. I believe, and I thank You for it, Father. In the Name of Jesus Christ, I pray. Amen.

The Book of Warfare Weapons
Chapter 41
Witnessing

Primary Purpose: Divine act, getting souls saved
Effective Use: Depression and wickedness
Strength: Extremely strong

Scriptures:

"But ye shall receive power, after that the Holy Ghost is come upon you: and ye shall be witnesses unto me both in Jerusalem, and in all Judaea, and in Samaria, and unto the uttermost parts of the earth" (Acts 1:8).

"Ye are my witnesses, saith the Lord, and my servant whom I have chosen: that ye may know and believe me, and understand that I am he: before me there was no God formed, neither shall there be after me" (Isaiah 43:10).

The Attack: You see people daily, but seldom do you tell anyone about Jesus. You don't want to bother people. You don't want to talk to them about Jesus because you don't know what to say or want to be rejected. You believe you will draw all people by merely letting your light shine but keeping your mouth closed. You know of people close to you who've died, and you never told them about Jesus. You don't believe there is a real Hell.

Weapon of Choice: Witnessing.

Defensively: This mighty weapon is in the divine class. It is effective against all peer pressure, shame, rejection, doubt, hatred, pride, malice, bondages, captivities, transgressions, and sins. It is especially effective against sin, addictions, habits, weakness, and depression.

Offensively: It is especially effective for reconciling men and women back to God. It is mighty for adding to the Kingdom of Heaven's population and adding names to the Lamb's Book of Life (Revelation 21:27).

Important Notes for this Weapon: Witnessing is encouraging others to accept Jesus Christ as their Lord and Savior. The primary use of this weapon is the divine act of getting souls saved. In addition, this weapon helps to promote the fact that eternal life is available to all people who are willing to receive it.

The Book of Warfare Weapons
Chapter 41
Witnessing

How to Use this Weapon: Start with prayer by asking the Holy Spirit to lead you to someone who needs to hear the gospel of Jesus Christ, which leads to salvation. Once you find the person, share with him or her the love of God. Focus on Jesus as the forgiver of sins and Savior of the world. We all were guilty of sins before God, but Jesus died on the cross to take away our sins and to give us eternal life. You may also want to get my CD training kit that teaches you how to witness with maximum impact, titled *"The Heaven Packing Power of Witnessing."* The Word says one planted, another watered, but God gave the increase (1 Corinthians 3:6). Remember, the angels in Heaven rejoice more over one sinner who repents than ninety-nine just persons who need no repentance (Luke 15:7). Give God thanksgiving and praise for the fantastic opportunity of being able to lead others to Jesus Christ.

Secrets of this Weapon: In the spirit realm, it is like you are on headline-breaking news for all of Heaven to watch as you go Witnessing. The angels in Heaven rejoice over one sinner that repents more than ninety-nine just persons who need no repentance (Luke 15:7 & 10). The active use of this weapon helps to offer eternal life to whomsoever is willing to receive it.

Weapon's Source of Power: The power energizing this weapon is the love of God, the Blood, and the life of Jesus Christ.

Faith Heroes Using this Weapon: Woman at the well (John 4:28-30); John the Baptist told Andrew (John 1:35-40); Andrew told Peter (John 1:41-42); Peter told Cornelius (Acts 10:19-48); Cornelius told and gathered his household (Acts 10:33); they told others (Acts 11:1); and Jesus has commanded us all to tell others, by sharing His gospel (Mark 16:15-16).

PICK YOUR CHALLENGE: For a more immersive experience pick your challenge below and complete it according to the instructions listed. For the best experience and maximum impact complete all activities, exercises, and challenges.

The Book of Warfare Weapons
Chapter 41
Witnessing

Your Challenge: Make a list of ten people to whom you will witness about Jesus Christ. Pray and ask the Holy Spirit to help you do it.

For A Great Challenge: Complete activities in Chapter #41 of *The Book of Warfare Weapons–Workbook*.

For A Group Challenge: Complete the Group Challenge of Chapter #41 of *The Book of Warfare Weapons–Workbook*.

For A Great Online Challenge: Complete the online activities and challenges in Chapter #41 of *The Book of Warfare Weapons–Outstanding Warrior Challenge (TBOWW-OWC) online challenge* at www.tbowowc.com.

Prayer of Activation: Father, I thank You so much for giving me the immense opportunity to be a witness of Your Gospel. Thank you for helping me share with the world benefits that you freely give them through Jesus Christ and the power of the Holy Spirit. Thank You for making me one of Your ambassadors. I am afforded the right, privilege, and authorization to share with all mankind the excellent news that they can live and not die. May I share with them the truth that they can have life and have it more abundantly, not only in this world but also in the eternal world which is to come. Help me to take Witnessing to heart. Help me to be bold in faith to share You with everyone I meet. Help me, through the love of God that is shed abroad in my heart, to connect with others through love. Help me introduce them to Your grace so that their names will be written in the Lamb's Book of Life. Please give me more grace now to be effective at Witnessing. Help me bear much fruit through the Holy Spirit. May my fruit remain forever. I give You thanks and praise, Father, believing that You are strengthening me to be an effective witness for You. In the Name of Jesus Christ, I pray. Amen.

The Book of Warfare Weapons
Chapter 42
The Church

Primary Purpose: Divine government on earth
Effective Use: All enemies and all things
Strength: Divine class

Scriptures:

"And hath put all things under his feet, and gave him to be the head over all things to the church" (Ephesians 1:22).

"That he might present it to himself a glorious church, not having spot, or wrinkle, or any such thing; but that it should be holy and without blemish" (Ephesians 5:27).

The Attack: You have never joined a church, or you are not faithful in attendance to the one you have joined. You believe you can serve God better at home. You think that churches are full of hypocrites or that they are only after your money. You don't like to fellowship or communicate with other believers. You feel that you are the only one living right. You believe in God and say He knows your heart to understand why church is not for you.

Weapon of Choice: The Church.

Defensively: This excellent and living weapon is in the divine class and is effective against all the enemy's powers.

Offensively: This weapon is God's ultimate plan throughout the ages, as revealed in Jesus Christ. It brings us into fellowship with God forever and ever (Revelation 21:3).

Important Notes for this Weapon: The Church is known as a place for worshipping God, for receiving encouragement, deliverance, training, development, and for fellowshipping with other believers. The Church is also the people who make up the members of a congregation. The primary purpose of the Church is to function as God's representative form of government on earth, fulfilling the Father's divine will and promoting the Gospel of Jesus Christ. It is effective against all enemies and all things.

The Book of Warfare Weapons
Chapter 42
The Church

The number of people in each group is not as significant as the condition of their hearts. The Word says, "Where two or three are gathered together in my name, there am I in the midst of them" (Matthew 18:20).

How to Use this Weapon: Pray and ask the Holy Spirit to lead you to a church (a local assembly of believers) where the Word of God is taught, the cross of Jesus Christ is preached, the love of God is felt, faith is demonstrated, hope is proclaimed, grace abounds, all people are welcomed, and the Holy Spirit has the freedom to move as the Father wills. Most importantly, a place that makes Witnessing a top priority. Once you find such a church, join it as a member. Then, faithfully support it with your prayers, time, talents, and tithes.

Secrets of this Weapon: In the spirit realm, the Church is the true heir of salvation, a chosen generation, a royal priesthood, a holy nation – a whole kingdom of kings and priests (1 Peter 2:9 & and Revelation 1:6). Heaven belongs to the redeemed, and they will enjoy its pleasures for all eternity.

Weapon's Source of Power: This weapon's source of power is the body of Jesus Christ, of which He is the Head.

Faith Heroes Using this Weapon: The church at Jerusalem (Acts 11:22); the church at Antioch (Acts 13:1); the church at Cenchrea (Romans 16:1); the small church in the house of Priscilla (wife) and husband Aquila (Romans 16:3-5 and Acts 18:1-4, 18, 24-26); the seven churches of Asia (Revelation Chapters 1-3); and many more.

PICK YOUR CHALLENGE: For a more immersive experience pick your challenge below and complete it according to the instructions listed. For the best experience and maximum impact complete all activities, exercises, and challenges.

The Book of Warfare Weapons
Chapter 42
The Church

Your Challenge: The challenge is to become a member of a church or become active in your church. Commit to attending church twice a week, volunteering at church, or bringing ten people to church.

For A Great Challenge: Complete activities in Chapter #42 of *The Book of Warfare Weapons–Workbook.*

For A Group Challenge: Complete the Group Challenge of Chapter #42 of *The Book of Warfare Weapons–Workbook.*

For A Great Online Challenge: Complete the online activities and challenges in Chapter #42 of *The Book of Warfare Weapons–Outstanding Warrior Challenge (TBOWW-OWC) online challenge at* www.tbowowc.com.

Prayer of Activation: Our Father, I thank You for sending Jesus, who is the head of the church. I thank You, Father, that You have placed me in the church and the body of Christ as it has pleased You. I thank You that You have allowed me to connect to a local body of believers in a local church. You said that we are not to forsake the assembling of ourselves together, and this local church that You have allowed me to connect to is a great blessing – a heavenly, divine blessing on the earth. Help me defend it, support it, encourage it, share it with others, and invite others to it. Help us to be the church not by mere form but by living out the realities of Your Word. Allow me to submit to authority while also walking in authority. Help me to be an accurate reflection of the life of Christ on the earth. Help me not give in to peer pressure or societal influences that would cause me to be disloyal to Your Holy Spirit, eternal Word, or heavenly council. Give me boldness so that I may stand for righteousness, truth, love, and grace. I thank You that I will accomplish all You have called me to achieve in the church through the Holy Spirit. I believe and thank You for it, Father. In the Name of Jesus Christ, I pray. Amen.

The Book of Warfare Weapons
Chapter 43
Faith
Primary Purpose: Spiritual Substance to please God
Effective Use: Many enemies
Strength: Divine class

Scriptures:
"Now faith is the substance of things hoped for, the evidence of things not seen" (Hebrews 11:1).
"For therein is the righteousness of God revealed from faith to faith: as it is written, The just shall live by faith" (Romans 1:17).
"But without faith it is impossible to please him: for he that cometh to God must believe that he is and that he is a rewarder of them that diligently seek him" (Hebrews 11:6).

The Attack: You are in need. You are in want. The desires of your heart are unfulfilled. You are experiencing lack. You are experiencing opposition, trouble, or have suffered a loss. You have been hurt, disappointed, betrayed, falsely accused, misused, or mishandled, but for some reason, you keep going. What is that thing inside you that keeps pushing you forward and refuses to allow you to quit?

Weapon of Choice: Faith.

Defensively: This excellent and living weapon is in the divine class and is effective against all the enemy's powers.

Offensively: This weapon pleases God greatly. It enables one to walk in unlimited power and maintain a good rapport with God (Hebrews 11:2).

Important Notes for this Weapon: Faith is the spiritual, "God-kind of substance" that God used to create all things in existence. This spiritual substance is so explosively powerful that it can make anything possible. Jesus used it when He framed the world. Because of the love, goodness, and the Grace of God, He has given us the authority and privilege of using this same spiritual "God-kind of substance" to frame our lives.

The Book of Warfare Weapons
Chapter 43
Faith

This Faith enables a believer to walk in dominion, authority, power, and continual victory. It also allows a person to tap into the miracle-working power of God. Faith comes directly from the Word of God. The more you hear, receive, and believe the Word, the more Faith will come alive within your heart.

How to Use this Weapon: Listen to or read the Word of God. Receive it as being the absolute truth of God, then believe it to the point of obeying it.

Secrets of this Weapon: The creative spiritual "God-kind" of substance that comes by the Word of God. It is so potent that it can enable a person to flow in the God-kind of miraculous power with miracles, signs, and wonders following.

Weapon's Source of Power: The Word of God.

Faith Heroes Using this Weapon: Many heroes are listed in the Heroes Hall of Faith (Hebrews 11) and used by all saints in every generation that desires to please God.

PICK YOUR CHALLENGE: For a more immersive experience pick your challenge below and complete it according to the instructions listed.
For the best experience and maximum impact complete all activities, exercises, and challenges.

Your Challenge: List five areas of your life where you can exercise Faith to change your course in life. Explain how?

For A Great Challenge: Complete activities in Chapter #43 of *The Book of Warfare Weapons–Workbook.*

For A Group Challenge: Complete the Group Challenge of Chapter #43 of *The Book of Warfare Weapons–Workbook.*

The Book of Warfare Weapons
Chapter 43
Faith

For A Great Online Challenge: Complete the online activities and challenges in Chapter #43 of *The Book of Warfare Weapons–Outstanding Warrior Challenge (TBOWW-OWC) online challenge at* <u>www.tbowowc.com</u>.

Prayer of Activation: Father, I give You thanks and praise that through Jesus Christ, I have Faith. I thank You because You said if I have Faith the size of a mustard seed, I can say to a mountain, "Be thou removed, and be cast into the sea; and shall not doubt in my heart, but shall believe that those things which I say shall come to pass; I shall have whatsoever I say" (Mark 11:23). I thank You that the Faith You have given me is well able to please You. I pray that the Faith You have delivered to me will increase through and by Your power and through listening and partaking of Your Word. Help me to walk before You full of Faith because I know this is what You desire of me. By Faith, I believe that I shall fulfill the purpose you've called me to achieve on the earth. I thank You for it, Father. In the Name of Jesus Christ, I pray. Amen.

The Book of Warfare Weapons
Chapter 44
Hope
Primary Purpose: Strength of endurance
Effective Use: Anxiety and discouragement
Strength: Divine class

Scriptures:
"And hope maketh not ashamed; because the love of God is shed abroad in our hearts by the Holy Ghost which is given unto us" (Romans 5:5). "The Lord taketh pleasure in them that fear him, in those that hope in his mercy" (Psalm 147:11). "Now the God of hope fill you with all joy and peace in believing, that ye may abound in hope, through the power of the Holy Ghost" (Romans 15:13).

The Attack: The enemy is telling you that this is the end. There is no way out. Things will only get worse. Stop now while you are ahead. You want to quit and walk away, but you still believe that somehow or in some way, things can change.

Weapon of Choice: Hope.

Defensively: This weapon is in the divine class and is effective against all powers of the enemy, especially against depression, anxiety, hopelessness, and suicidal ideation.

Offensively: This weapon brings strength, refreshing, encouragement, motivation, joy, peace, and rejoicing.

Important Notes for this Weapon: The Weapon of Hope is great for times when things are going wrong or the odds are stacked against you. It is most effective when all your circumstances appear unfavorable to you. The primary purpose of Hope is to give a person the strength of endurance. Hope is relentless optimism that refuses to quit because it has confidence in God. Hope answers the never-ending "ability of God" question. The question that rhetorically asks, "Can God?" The answer, as declared by Hope, is "God Can!!!" God asked Abraham, "Abraham, is there anything too hard for God?" Hope proclaims, "There is nothing too hard for God!"

The Book of Warfare Weapons
Chapter 44
Hope

How to Use this Weapon: You use this weapon by realizing that no situation is hopeless. You activate Hope by considering the truth that God can change any situation concerning you, and more importantly, He wants to do so. No matter what you experience in life, God is able to turn it around in a moment. Release Hope by speaking it into situations. When you speak Hope into a situation, Hope will come on the scene and defend you.

Secrets of this Weapon: In the spirit realm, it is like you are receiving a river of optimism from God. The more it flows, the more it strengthens you so that you refuse to quit.

Weapon's Source of Power: This weapon is energized by the mercy and goodness of God.

Faith Heroes Using this Weapon: Hannah (1 Samuel 1:6-20); Sarah (Hebrews 11:11); Man at the pool of Bethsaida (John 5); Abraham (Romans 4:18); Noah (Genesis 6:12-7:16); and many others.

PICK YOUR CHALLENGE: For a more immersive experience pick your challenge below and complete it according to the instructions listed. For the best experience and maximum impact complete all activities, exercises, and challenges.

Your Challenge: Think about areas in your life where you need to experience breakthroughs. Make confessions of Hope in God and declare His great power and ability to bring you out.

For A Great Challenge: Complete activities in Chapter #44 of *The Book of Warfare Weapons–Workbook.*

For A Group Challenge: Complete the Group Challenge of Chapter #44 of *The Book of Warfare Weapons–Workbook.*

The Book of Warfare Weapons
Chapter 44
Hope

For A Great Online Challenge: Complete the online activities and challenges in Chapter #44 of *The Book of Warfare Weapons–Outstanding Warrior Challenge (TBOWW-OWC) online challenge at* <u>www.tbowowc.com</u>.

Prayer of Activation: Father, thank You so much that You have given me Hope. Regardless of what I've experienced in life, tomorrow shall be a better day. I believe that things are getting better for me. I believe that more incredible things are yet to come. My Hope rests on Your Word that declares, "I will never leave you or forsake you. I will be with you always even until the end of the world." I pray that You help me keep my eyes on You, Jesus as the Author and Finisher of my faith. I pray, Heavenly Father, through Your Holy Spirit, that You'll help me to connect my faith to my Hope. For it is written, "For hope maketh not ashamed as the love of God is shed abroad in my heart." I thank You, dear God, that through Your Word, You let us know that You're coming back for Your people in a moment, in the twinkling of an eye. Wherefore, we are to encourage one another with this Hope. We know that in the end, we will walk in complete victory. Help me to continue to keep my eyes upon You and not on the circumstances around me in this temporal world. For, in the end, we will rule and reign with You, as we hold on to Hope by faith. The reward of holding on to Hope is that we may receive a crown of life in the end. Thank You for giving me hope that will stay with me and continually increase all the days of my life. Thank You, Father. In the Name of Jesus Christ, I pray. Amen.

The Book of Warfare Weapons
Chapter 45
Love
Primary Purpose: Greatest of all powers
Effective Use: All enemies and all things
Strength: Divine class

Scriptures:
"He that loveth not knoweth not God; for God is love" (1 John 4:8).
"And we have known and believed the love that God hath to us. God is love; and he that dwelleth in love dwelleth in God, and God in him" (1 John 4:16).
"Owe no man anything, but to love one another: for he that loveth another hath fulfilled the law" (Romans 13:8).

The Attack: You hate someone who wronged you, who you don't understand, or who you envy. You hate someone of a different nationality, race, or religion. You feel that other people are inferior to you, that you are better than others. You are full of worry, anxiety, and often battle fear. You don't like most people and find it difficult to trust others. You are suspicious of everyone, and few can measure up to your expectations except you. You only think about what is good for you or what will benefit you.

Weapon of Choice: Love.

Defensively: This excellent and living weapon is in the divine class. It is one of the greatest of all weapons, as it is God. For God does not merely have love, but He is Love. Therefore, it is effective against everything in creation that opposes it.

Offensively: The power contained in this weapon is so immense that continuous use of it transforms an individual into the image of Jesus Christ by the power of the Holy Spirit (2 Corinthians 3:18).

Important Notes for this Weapon: It is the greatest of all powers. Love is the life force of God. It is the exact composition of God. Love comes from no other place in the universe except God. The actual litmus test of all authentic and genuine children of God is having God's nature. The nature of God is Love. Love is the greatest weapon. Love is also a law.

The Book of Warfare Weapons
Chapter 45
Love

It is the supreme law, and it has the highest authority over all laws in Heaven, earth, or under the earth. Love is also God's greatest commandment: "Thou shall love the Lord thy God with all thy heart, mind, soul, and strength." The second great commandment: "Thou shall love thy neighbor as thyself." These two greatest commandments fulfill all the Bible's teachings in the law and through prophets (Mark 12:30-31). Love is also a spirit. God has not given us the spirit of fear, but (*He has given us the spirit*) of Love, power, and a sound mind (2 Timothy 1:7).

The most significant experience of life is to live entirely devoted to the spirit of Love of God in Christ Jesus. You will then know, by revelation and from experience, the ancient Love that Christ has, which of itself surpasses knowledge and can fill you with all the fullness of God (Ephesians 3:19). NOTE: We are focusing on Agape Love, which is perfect or divine Love. The other Greeks terms for Love: Philia, Eros, Pragma, Ludus, or Philautia, are all imperfect. They will all shift, change, or fail in the process of time. Only Agape Love will remain immutable and enduring for all eternity.

How to Use this Weapon: Ask God to fill you with the Spirit of Love in the Name of Jesus Christ. The Spirit of Love will then teach you its ways, which are the ways of God.

Secrets of this Weapon: In the spirit realm, it's like you will have tapped into the life force of God. As you allow the Spirit of Love to transform you into the image of Jesus Christ, it will then escort you into the divine fellowship of Love between the Father, Jesus Christ the Son, and the Holy Spirit.

Weapon's Source of Power: This weapon is energized by Love. Love is its own power. Love is God, and God is Love.

Faith Heroes Using this Weapon: The greatest example is Jesus Christ (John 3:16 & 15:12-14); Ruth (1:16-18); Jonathan (1 Samuel 18:1); Stephen (Acts 7:55-60); Mary (Luke 7:36-47) and many more.

The Book of Warfare Weapons
Chapter 45
Love

PICK YOUR CHALLENGE: For a more immersive experience pick your challenge below and complete it according to the instructions listed.
For the best experience and maximum impact complete all activities, exercises, and challenges.

Your Challenge: Make a list of ten people to whom you can begin to show Love. Commit to ten ways of showing love to others.

For A Great Challenge: Complete activities in Chapter #45 of *The Book of Warfare Weapons–Workbook.*

For A Group Challenge: Complete the Group Challenge of Chapter #45 of *The Book of Warfare Weapons–Workbook.*

For A Great Online Challenge: Complete the online activities and challenges in Chapter #45 of *The Book of Warfare Weapons–Outstanding Warrior Challenge (TBOWW-OWC) online challenge at* www.tbowowc.com.

Chapter 45
Love

Prayer of Activation: My Father, I thank You for loving us so much that You gave us Jesus Christ. "For God so loved the world that He gave His only begotten Son, that whosoever believeth in Him should not perish but have everlasting life" (John 3:16). "Herein is Love, not that we Love You, but that You first loved us, and gave Your life for our ransom" (1 John 4:10). I Thank You, God, that Your Love is shed abroad in our hearts. I reject all hate, anger and rage, and everything that goes against Love. I cast them away from me in the Name of Jesus Christ. I accept the Love of God that makes us perfect and enables us to live in complete fellowship with You. I pray that Your Love, which You have placed within my heart, will increase exponentially and that I will be known as a person of Love. I will do everything I do through and by the power of Your Love that will lead me, guide me, and direct me in all aspects of life. I thank You that I was meant to live a life of Love. I will obey Love, and I will do whatever Love will instruct me to do. I believe that I now receive the Love of God. Thank you, Father. In the Name of Jesus Christ, I pray. Amen.

The Book of Warfare Weapons
Chapter 46
Testimonies
Primary Purpose: Bragging on God
Effective Use: All enemies, especially the devil
Strength: Extremely strong

Scriptures:
"And they overcame him by the blood of the Lamb, and by the word of their testimony; and they loved not their lives unto the death" (Revelation 12:11).
"Who bare record of the word of God, and of the testimony of Jesus Christ, and of all things that he saw" (Revelation 1:2).

The Attack: You rarely tell others what God has done for you because you tell yourself that you want to stay humble. You feel others will not accept or believe your testimony anyway. You feel you don't want anyone to know your past struggle because they may think less of you. You think that sharing how you overcame your past struggles is a waste of time or that it only happened by chance, luck, or fortune. You are doubtful that it was God who did it for you. You think that you got to your place in life all by yourself, and God had nothing to do with it.

Weapon of Choice: Testimonies.

Defensively: This mighty weapon is effective against all the powers of the enemy, especially for overcoming Satan.

Offensively: This weapon is excellent for spreading faith and for replicating and duplicating victories to all who will hear and believe them.

Important Notes for this Weapon: This weapon releases the miraculous power of God to give you victory. In its most basic form, a testimony is simply sharing with someone about a past victory that Jesus gave to you. In its advanced form, a testimony is bragging on God to such an extent that the power of faith, demonstrated in a past victory, comes on the scene again, to give you or the hearer a new victory similar to the previous one. Thus, each time that you give a testimony, you are giving honor and glory to God.

The Book of Warfare Weapons
Chapter 46
Testimonies

How to Use this Weapon: Think about a time God gave you a victory, and you knew it was only God. Think of how great it made you feel. Also, think of what would have happened if God did not come through for you. Now, out of gratitude and appreciation, share that testimony with someone. Note: In your testimony, focus less on yourself or the problems caused by the enemy, and focus more on what Jesus has done. A true testimony will help other people see Jesus amid all the details of you sharing the life event.

Secrets of this Weapon: In the spirit realm, it's like faith comes on the scene again to give all the hearers of the testimony the same victory if they are willing to believe. In Matthew 9:20, the woman with the issue of blood was the first to touch the hem of Jesus' garment, and she was made whole. She testified before the multitude that her healing came by touching the hem of His garment. Then, in Matthew 14:36, others came also and touched the hem of His garment, and as many as touched it were made whole.

Weapon's Source of Power: The Glory of God, filled to the overflow with wonder-working power, is the source behind testimonies. When a person testifies, giving honor to Jesus, he becomes eligible to receive a measure of power that comes from the Glory that surrounds God.

Faith Heroes Using this Weapon: Woman at the well (John 4:28-30, 39); the man blind from birth (John 9:1-34); the Shunammite woman (2 Kings 8:1-6); Mary (Luke 1:35-56); Paul (Acts 26); and many others.

PICK YOUR CHALLENGE: For a more immersive experience pick your challenge below and complete it according to the instructions listed. For the best experience and maximum impact complete all activities, exercises, and challenges.

Your Challenge: Share your testimony of salvation with five people this week.

The Book of Warfare Weapons
Chapter 46
Testimonies

For A Great Challenge: Complete activities in Chapter #46 of *The Book of Warfare Weapons–Workbook*.

For A Group Challenge: Complete the Group Challenge of Chapter #46 of *The Book of Warfare Weapons–Workbook*.

For A Great Online Challenge: Complete the online activities and challenges in Chapter #46 of *The Book of Warfare Weapons–Outstanding Warrior Challenge (TBOWW-OWC) online challenge* at www.tbowowc.com.

Prayer of Activation: Father, I thank You that You have given us the wonderful privilege of using Testimonies to advance Your kingdom in a great and mighty way. Testimonies allow us to see Your power, strength, and might manifest in our lives. You use them to reveal wisdom and for Your love to manifest to defeat the enemy at every turn. Through Your faith, we offer praise and honor in remembrance of the great things You have done. Help me to be more faithful in testifying of all the good things You have done. Help me look back and remember all the times You have brought me out, delivered me, healed me, rescued me, or set me free. In each one of those instances, Your power and Your Grace were made manifest. The same Grace and power will always come on the scene when I call to remembrance of what You have done. Testimonies of Your works defeat the enemy continually. For even the Bible says that we overcome him – the enemy – by the Blood of the Lamb and the word of our testimony (Revelation 12:11). Help me to always keep a testimony in my mouth. Help me always be quick to tell of Your goodness and encourage others along this journey of life. I believe that You will give me more extraordinary Testimonies to defeat and to have victory over the enemy. I believe that I now receive more incredible Testimonies by faith. I believe that my Testimonies will bring You honor and glory. Thank You for it, Father. In the Name of Jesus Christ, I pray. Amen.

The Book of Warfare Weapons
Chapter 47
The Blood of Jesus

Primary Purpose: Divine act, brings many blessings
Effective Use: All enemies; protection
Strength: Divine class

Scriptures:

"And he took the cup, and gave thanks, and gave it to them, saying, *Drink ye all of it; For this is my blood of the new testament, which is shed for many for the remission of sins*" (Matthew 26:27-28). "And they overcame him by the blood of the Lamb, and by the word of their testimony; and they loved not their lives unto the death" (Revelation 12:11).

The Attack: You are a sinner and need your sins forgiven. You are under spiritual attack and want victory. You are a new convert and want to claim your birthright inheritance. You are a saint who wants to grow in the things of God. You are administering deliverance to one possessed by a demon. You are activating protection for yourself or others. There are countless other reasons, and situations too numerous to mention, where the Blood of Jesus is to be applied.

Weapon of Choice: The Blood of Jesus.

Defensively: This excellent and living weapon is in the divine class. It is effective against all the powers of the enemy.

Offensively: It is especially effective for salvation, deliverance, protection, health, recovery, and providing legal access to all the blessings of Heaven through Jesus Christ.

Important Notes for this Weapon: The Blood of Jesus is so perfect and powerful that it is the only substance in all creation that can destroy sin and wash away the stains of sin. The Blood of Jesus covers every aspect of our lives. By the Blood of Jesus, we have forgiveness, atonement, regeneration, redemption, transformation, sanctification, purification, glorification, justification, protection, adoption, completion, unity, grace, mercy, and more privileges, honors, blessings, gifts, callings, benefits, and promises than we can name.

The Book of Warfare Weapons
Chapter 47
The Blood of Jesus

How to Use this Weapon: There is an unlimited number of ways to use this weapon. One of the most common is to boldly proclaim it in the face of danger, confusion, oppression, depression, or spiritual attack. Simply declare, "Satan, the Blood of Jesus is against you!!!" "I resist you with the Blood of Jesus." The enemy can't stand you reminding him of the Blood of Jesus, for the Blood of Jesus is the enemy's greatest defeat, but it is your greatest victory!

Secrets of this Weapon: In the spirit realm, the Blood of Jesus is so many things to us. One thing of the many things is the realization that the Blood of Jesus is like our Bill of Rights for the Constitution of Heaven.

Weapon's Source of Power: The Life of Jesus Christ poured out for our use. The Blood of Jesus is so powerful that it is beyond our comprehension. All other blood dries up and dies once they leave the body, but the Blood of Jesus remains wet and very much alive today. All other blood gets weak and breaks down over time, but the Blood of Jesus remains strong and never loses its power. All other blood can not speak, but the Blood of Jesus will speak on your behalf. You must protect all other blood, but the Blood of Jesus protects you. Other blood can only secure identification with one's biological father, but the Blood of Jesus secures fellowship with our Heavenly Father. The Blood of Jesus can be applied to every situation in life to get you to victory.

Faith Heroes Using this Weapon: Every saint everywhere partakes of the Blood of Jesus. "Then Jesus said unto them, *"Verily, verily, I say unto you, Except ye eat the flesh of the Son of man, and drink his blood, ye have no life in you"* (John 6:53).

The Book of Warfare Weapons
Chapter 47
The Blood of Jesus

PICK YOUR CHALLENGE: For a more immersive experience pick your challenge below and complete it according to the instructions listed.
For the best experience and maximum impact complete all activities, exercises, and challenges.

Your Challenge: The next time trouble arises, declare the Blood of Jesus against it.

For A Great Challenge: Complete activities in Chapter #47 of *The Book of Warfare Weapons–Workbook*.

For A Group Challenge: Complete the Group Challenge of Chapter #47 of *The Book of Warfare Weapons–Workbook*.

For A Great Online Challenge: Complete the online activities and challenges in Chapter #47 of *The Book of Warfare Weapons–Outstanding Warrior Challenge (TBOWW-OWC) online challenge at* _www.tbowowc.com_.

Prayer of Activation: Father, I thank You so much that You allowed Jesus to offer up His own Blood so our sins may be remitted and forgiven. Thank You that through the Blood of Jesus, we have eternal life. Thank You that through the shedding of the Blood of Jesus, we are adopted into Your royal family, and have become children of the Most High God. I pray, Father, that the revelation of the Blood of Jesus would always be made manifest within me. I pray that I will always realize that in addition to salvation, it is also given for my protection, strength, healing, and my life. Everything I need for abundant life is wrapped up in the Blood of Jesus. Help me always to have faith in the Blood of Jesus. Help me, continually, to draw from its strength and power to defeat the powers of the enemy. Help me to walk in the refreshing that only the Blood of Jesus can bring. Father, I thank You for it. In the Name of Jesus Christ, I pray. Amen.

143

The Book of Warfare Weapons
Chapter 48
Name of Jesus Christ
Primary Purpose: Divine act, brings many blessings
Effective Use: All enemies and all things
Strength: Divine class

Scriptures:

"Wherefore God also hath highly exalted him, and given him a name which is above every name: that at the name of Jesus every knee should bow, of things in heaven, and things in earth, and things under the earth; And that every tongue should confess that Jesus Christ is Lord, to the glory of God the Father" (Philippians 2:9-11).

"And she shall bring forth a son, and thou shalt call his name JESUS: for he shall save his people from their sins" (Matthew 1:21).

"Neither is there salvation in any other: for there is none other name under heaven given among men, whereby we must be saved" (Acts 4:12).

The Attack: You are a sinner and need to be saved. You are saved but are living a carnal life. You think it doesn't matter if you refuse the Name of Jesus, as long as you believe in God. You would use the Name of Jesus, but you don't want to offend anyone. You would use the Name of Jesus, but you don't want to be persecuted. You believe that there is nothing special about the Name of Jesus, only the life He lived. You need help, protection, guidance, healing, or a breakthrough. You are under spiritual attack and need to exercise power. You want to access all your spiritual benefits and blessings from Heaven. You want to receive Baptism in the Holy Spirit. It brings more blessings, privileges, honors, gifts, callings, promises, and benefits than we can name.

Weapon of Choice: The Name of Jesus Christ.

Defensively: This excellent and living weapon is in the divine class. It is effective against all the powers of the enemy.

Offensively: It is especially effective for accessing all the blessings, graces, favor, wisdom, weapons, gifts, authority, and powers of Heaven.

The Book of Warfare Weapons
Chapter 48
Name of Jesus Christ

Important Notes for this Weapon: The Name of Jesus is a divine act of God that He revealed upon the Earth. In eternity past, Jesus had many titles but no name. He was universally known as the Word of God. Because He created all things, and all things were made by Him, (John 1:3). He made all things, and all things knew Him. There was no need to give Himself a name until the time of the fall of mankind. There was no need until the time He revealed His greatest artistic masterpiece of the ages called redemption. In redemption, He would create man. Man would fall to sin. Sin would blind the eyes, understanding, and heart of man. Man would lose consciousness, knowledge, and the awareness of God. God would reintroduce Himself to mankind by sending His only begotten Son (the WORD). The WORD is the expressed image of the invisible God and is equal to the Father (Hebrews 1:3). While the WORD walked on the earth in human flesh, God the Father gave the WORD, the name JESUS, as spoken by the angel to his mother Mary (Matthew 1:21). He kept the name JESUS until the resurrection. Let me explain; it was decided in eternity past (before the world was) that Jesus (the WORD) would accomplish the masterpiece of redemption. It was at the spiritual awards ceremony called the resurrection of Jesus that God awarded Jesus (the WORD) with the greatest honor of all. God raised Jesus from the dead and exalted His Name even higher than before (even to the highest point in Heaven). At that elevation and glorification, God added the term CHRIST to the name JESUS. The exalted Name of JESUS CHRIST is HIS Glorified new name (after the resurrection), which speaks to His Eternal work of Redemption (reconciling mankind back to God) and to His triumph over sin, Satan, death, hell, the grave, the flesh, and the world. Therefore, to honor His Son JESUS CHRIST, God made his name higher than every name in Heaven, on earth, or under the earth (Philippians 2:9-11). The Name of JESUS is higher than the heavenly names of Elohim, Jehovah, Jehovah-Jireh, El Shaddai, or Jehovah-Rapha. All these names spoke to Old Testament covenants and promises, but none of those covenants or promises are more honored than the covenant, God made by

The Book of Warfare Weapons
Chapter 48
Name of Jesus Christ

the Blood of JESUS CHRIST – the covenant and promise of redemption. The Name of JESUS CHRIST includes all the benefits, blessings, promises, and covenants of the Old Testament and unlimited blessings, promises, and powers of the New Testament, which are built on better promises (Hebrews 8:6). Therefore, when you call on the Name of JESUS CHRIST, you are calling on the highest power and highest authority established by God to honor His beloved Son, JESUS CHRIST's eternal work of redemption.

NOTE: Jesus has lots of titles (King of Kings, Prince of Peace, Bread of Heaven, Lion of Tribe of Judah, Lamb of God, "and many more-too numerous more to list all here"), but one name; "JESUS CHRIST" (Acts 2:38; 3:6; 3:20; 4:10; 5:42; 8:12; 8:37; 10:36; Acts 16:18; and many more). The person JESUS CHRIST fulfills all titles, honors, majesty, dominion, authorities, wisdom, might, strength, and power of God.

How to Use this Weapon: Simply open your mouth and call on JESUS CHRIST. He will hear you. The more you call Him, the more power will be released from Heaven to you and through you. There is nothing wrong with calling on the Name of JESUS CHRIST. It is our highest badge of honor because of the blessings of redemption.

Secrets of this Weapon: In the spirit realm, the Name of JESUS CHRIST brings you into the throne room of God or the secret chambers of the Most High God. It is as if you have received authority, power, and special access to visit the White House or Buckingham Palace at will, so it is in the spirit. You have been given special access by God, and you are accepted in the Heavenly Kingdom as a VIP and most honored friend of JESUS CHRIST, the King of Heaven. Your level of access when using the Name of JESUS CHRIST will depend upon the degree that which you love God from your heart in true obedience unto Him.

Every time you say the Name of JESUS CHRIST, you are acknowledging the birth, life, death, burial, resurrection, ascension, and glorification of

The Book of Warfare Weapons
Chapter 48
Name of Jesus Christ

JESUS CHRIST. He suffered greatly to restore us into fellowship with the Father through the act of redemption. Calling on the Name of JESUS CHRIST speaks to His victory, His honor, and His Glory!

Calling the Name of JESUS CHRIST is the highest honor placed upon man's lips by which a human can speak to the wisdom, power, and victory of CHRIST's atoning work of redemption.

Weapon's Source of Power: The Name of JESUS CHRIST has power in itself to save, heal, deliver, rescue, set free, restore, strengthen, unify, forgive, promote, protect, produce, energize, defend, re-align, calibrate, balance, guide, and resurrect all who put their trust in it.

Faith Heroes Using this Weapon: Peter (Acts 3:16); Ananias (Acts 9:17); Philip (Acts 8:12); Paul (Philippians 2:10 and Colossians 3:17); and many more.

PICK YOUR CHALLENGE: For a more immersive experience pick your challenge below and complete it according to the instructions listed.

For the best experience and maximum impact complete all activities, exercises, and challenges.

Your Challenge: Spend time giving God thanks and praise for giving us the Name of JESUS CHRIST. Spend time calling on the Name of Jesus Christ.

For A Great Challenge: Complete activities in Chapter #48 of *The Book of Warfare Weapons—Workbook.*

For A Group Challenge: Complete the Group Challenge of Chapter #48 of *The Book of Warfare Weapons—Workbook.*

For A Great Online Challenge: Complete the online activities and challenges in Chapter #48 of *The Book of Warfare Weapons—Outstanding Warrior Challenge (TBOWW-OWC)* online challenge at www.tbowowc.com.

The Book of Warfare Weapons
Chapter 48
Name of Jesus Christ

Prayer of Activation: Heavenly Father, I thank You that You have given Jesus Christ– The Living Word – a Name that is above every name in Heaven, on earth, and under the earth. I thank You that every blessing of grace is wrapped up in the Name of Jesus Christ. The exalted Name of Jesus Christ brings salvation, health, healing, wholeness, protection, defense, and so much more. Every blessing comes through the Name of Jesus Christ. I thank You for that glorious Name that You allow us to abide in. Whenever we exercise our faith in the Name of Jesus Christ, it connects us to His eternal work on the Cross. May I always have faith in the Name of Jesus Christ. May I never use His name in vain or in any dishonorable way. May I use it with the greatest of honor and reverence when calling upon it. I believe that I shall increase in faith and into the full measure of Christ as I abide in His holy Name. I believe that revelation of the Name of Jesus Christ shall increase within me like never before. I believe that I now receive a greater measure of faith in the Name of Jesus Christ. I thank You for it, Father. In the Name of Jesus Christ, I pray. Amen.

The Book of Warfare Weapons
Chapter 49
Baptism in the Holy Spirit

Primary Purpose: Divine act – brings many blessings
Effective Use: All enemies and all things
Strength: Divine class

Scriptures:

"And they were all filled with the Holy Ghost, and began to speak with other tongues, as the Spirit gave them utterance" (Acts 2:4).

"For John truly baptized with water; but ye shall be baptized with the Holy Ghost not many days hence" (Acts 1:5).

"And when Paul had laid his hands upon them, the Holy Ghost came on them; and they spake with tongues, and prophesied" (Acts 19:6).

The Attack: You are living the life of an ordinary person, and you have no spiritual power. You are a believer, but habits, yokes, or addictions bind you. You want the promised blessing of God's power. You don't know your God-given purpose on Earth. You don't know your spiritual gift. You are hungry for more of God. You want to live a life controlled by the Holy Spirit. You want to experience a revival from God followed by miracles, signs, and wonders. You want to be fruitful in spreading the gospel of Jesus Christ with boldness and effectiveness. It brings more blessings, privileges, honors, gifts, callings, promises, and benefits than we can name.

Weapon of Choice: Baptism in the Holy Spirit.

Defensively: This excellent and living weapon is in the divine class. It is effective against all the powers of the enemy.

Offensively: It is the Holy Spirit dwelling within the believer to fulfill the will of God. It is especially effective for enabling a believer to transition from being a mere professor of Christ to being a possessor of all the power of God through Jesus Christ.

Important Notes for this Weapon: Baptism in the Holy Spirit is essential for the success of every believer. Jesus Christ was intentional when He told His disciples that they were not to depart from Jerusalem until they were

The Book of Warfare Weapons
Chapter 49
Baptism in the Holy Spirit

baptized in the Holy Ghost. He said they would receive power after the Holy Spirit came upon them. This power is necessary to overcome all the power of the enemy that would seek to oppose you (Luke 10:19). The results of this baptism will bring to you, and activate within you, your spiritual gifts.

How to Use this Weapon: Ask the Father to fill you with the Baptism of the Holy Spirit in Jesus Christ Name. Believe that He hears you, and then receive it by faith. Now give God continual thanks and praise, believing that it will manifest.

Secrets of this Weapon: In the spirit realm, when you fully yield yourself in obedience to God, the Holy Spirit then comes and fills you with power and gifts to the overflow.

Weapon's Source of Power: The power of this weapon comes directly from the Holy Spirit.

Faith Heroes Using this Weapon: Elisabeth (Luke 1:41); 120 disciples (Acts 2:1-4); their company (Acts 4:23, 31); Peter (Acts 2:38-39); Paul (Acts 9:17); Stephen, Philip, Prochorus, Nicanor, Timon, Parmenas, and Nicolas (Acts 6:5); and many others. Jesus Christ wants you also to receive the Baptism in the Holy Spirit (John 14:16, 26, 15:26, 16:13).

PICK YOUR CHALLENGE: For a more immersive experience pick your challenge below and complete it according to the instructions listed. For the best experience and maximum impact complete all activities, exercises, and challenges.

Your Challenge: Have you been baptized in the Holy Spirit? By faith, ask Jesus Christ to baptize you in the Holy Spirit.

For A Great Challenge: Complete activities in Chapter #49 of *The Book of Warfare Weapons–Workbook.*

The Book of Warfare Weapons
Chapter 49
Baptism in the Holy Spirit

For A Group Challenge: Complete the Group Challenge of Chapter #49 of *The Book of Warfare Weapons–Workbook.*

For A Great Online Challenge: Complete the online activities and challenges in Chapter #49 of *The Book of Warfare Weapons–Outstanding Warrior Challenge (TBOWW-OWC)* at www.tbowowc.com.

Prayer of Activation: Holy Father, I thank You for giving us the promise of Your Holy Spirit. You have sent the Holy Spirit to give us the power to live the God-kind of life through faith in Jesus Christ. Thank You, sweet Jesus Christ, for You are the one who baptizes in the Holy Spirit with power and with fire. May You baptize me afresh, Lord Jesus Christ, with the Baptism in the Holy Spirit. May the power of the Highest come upon me. May I be able to flow in all the fullness of God to advance Your kingdom on the earth in a powerful way. For You said in the Book of Acts, *"But ye shall receive power, after that the Holy Ghost shall come upon you"* (Acts 1:8). Let the Holy Ghost come upon me, abide in me, and give me continual infillings of daily power. May You use my hands, feet, whole body, mind, and soul to fulfill Your will. May You live within me to fulfill the will of the Father on the earth. Your Word says that You will give the Holy Spirit to all who obey (Acts 5:32). I settled it in my heart to obey You by faith, through Your Grace. I believe that You shall Baptize me in the Holy Spirit. I believe that I receive it now in the Name of Jesus Christ. I believe that You shall give me the unique gift of speaking in tongues, which is Your heavenly language flowing out of my belly. May I be used of the Holy Spirit as an anointed, consecrated vessel to share the gospel of Jesus Christ with everyone I meet. I believe that I have received it. I thank You for it, Father. In the Name of Jesus Christ, I pray. Amen.

The Book of Warfare Weapons
Chapter 50
The Word of God

Primary Purpose: Divine act – brings many blessings
Effective Use: All enemies and all things
Strength: Divine class

Scriptures:
"In the beginning was the Word, and the Word was with God, and the Word was God. The same was in the beginning with God. All things were made by him; and without him was not any thing made that was made" (John 1:1-3). "And the Word was made flesh, and dwelt among us, (and we beheld his glory, the glory as of the only begotten of the Father,) full of grace and truth" (John 1:14).

The Attack: You do not know the Bible. You know a little about the Bible but can't quote any verses. You can quote the Bible but can't live it. Your prayers are weak. You don't know if what you are believing for is in God's will. You have experienced multiple disappointments and failures in life. You are looking for answers to life. You hunger for more of God. You want to grow in your knowledge and understanding of your faith walk. You want to renew your mind (and many other wants, desires, or needs, too numerous to list here).

Weapon of Choice: The Word of God.

Defensively: This excellent and living weapon is in the divine class. It is the greatest of all weapons, for it existed before all things, and all things in creation were made by it. It is effective in Heaven, on earth, under the earth, and over all things temporal and eternal. Therefore, the enemy does not stand a chance against the power of the Word.

Offensively: This weapon is so potent and powerful that there is nothing it cannot do when mixed with faith (John 1:1-3).

Important Notes for this Weapon: It is the divine, creative energy of life. It is the power inside all powers, revealed as the perfect unity of God and His Word as being one. It's a divine act that brings all blessings, including life. Consider this: The Word was manifest when nothing else was.

The Book of Warfare Weapons
Chapter 50
The Word of God

In other words, the Word was manifest when everything else was hidden or unseen. The Word then caused all things to appear and then hid Himself in unseen words. Yet, the Word of God is stronger than all that appears, for the unseen Word created it all. All things that appear are physically held together by the unseen power of the Word of God. The Word of God is revealed as all of God, expressed or manifested in one place, in the person of Jesus Christ. Please see my book titled *The Book of Warfare Strategies*. Refer to Chapter 4, "Sword of the Spirit," for a deeper understanding of this study.

How to Use this Weapon: Read the Word of God. Believe in the Word of God. Speak the Word of God. Live the Word of God.

Secrets of this Weapon: In the spirit realm, you are coming into the knowledge, wisdom, power, authority, truth, might, dominion, majesty, and training of God through the Word of God. It is as if you are sent to boot camp and are taught all things necessary to succeed in your new life as a soldier. The more of the Word you get into you, the more of the power of God will manifest through you. Therefore, meditate on this Word day and night, so shall you make your way prosperous, and you shall succeed (Joshua 1:8).

Weapon's Source of Power: The Word of God has the power within itself. Power is released by faith each time a person hears and believes the Word of God.

Faith Heroes Using this Weapon: The most excellent example is Jesus (Matthew 4, Luke 4). But, there are others also like Mary, Magdalene, Joanna, Mary mother of James, and other women (Luke 24:8-11 and John 2:22); David (1 Samuel 17:45-47); Paul (Romans 14:11, 1 Corinthians 1:19, Romans 3:10); Peter (Acts 3:22-26); Jude (Jude 14-15); Philip (Acts 8:26-35); and many others.

The Book of Warfare Weapons
Chapter 50
The Word of God

PICK YOUR CHALLENGE: For a more immersive experience pick your challenge below and complete it according to the instructions listed.
For the best experience and maximum impact complete all activities, exercises, and challenges.

Your Challenge: Make a plan to read through the Bible in one year.

For A Great Challenge: Complete activities in Chapter #50 of *The Book of Warfare Weapons–Workbook.*

For A Group Challenge: Complete the Group Challenge of Chapter #50 of *The Book of Warfare Weapons–Workbook.*

For A Great Online Challenge: Complete the online activities and challenges in Chapter #50 of *The Book of Warfare Weapons–Outstanding Warrior Challenge (TBOWW-OWC) online challenge at* <u>www.tbowowc.com</u>.

The Book of Warfare Weapons
Chapter 50
The Word of God

Prayer of Activation: Father, I thank You for giving us Your Word. We live by every word that proceeds out of Your mouth (Matthew 4:4). The more we read Your Word, speak Your Word, and obey Your Word, the more the life of Jesus Christ manifests within us (John 15:7-10). You told us to meditate on Your Word both day and night, and we shall make our way prosperous, and we shall have good success (Joshua 1:8). It will cause us to be fruitful in our season. You said if we abide in You, and Your Word abides in us, we shall ask what we will, and it shall be done. Let the full strength of Your Word be made manifest in my life. Help me to become a living epistle, seen and read by all men, as I hide Your Word in my heart that I might not sin against You (2 Corinthians 3:2 and Psalm 119:11). I love Your Word. I will read Your Word, devote myself to Your Word, and obey Your Word. I will seek to understand the truth of Your Word as Your Holy Spirit reveals it unto me. I thank You for the power of Your Word and ask that You help me be quick to conform to Your Word. I believe that by doing so, my profiting may appear before all (1 Timothy 4:15), and that great honor and glory may come to Your holy Name. I believe that I now receive a greater measure of grace for Your Word. I thank You for it, Father. In the Name of Jesus Christ, I pray. Amen.

ABOUT THE AUTHOR

Ezekiel Williams grew up in Ludowici, Georgia. He was very blessed in that his grandmother, father, and mother were all ministers of the Gospel of Jesus Christ. Ezekiel experienced his first "open vision" at age five during a Pentecostal revival meeting. From that point forward, he began to have unique experiences of visions, dreams, interpretation of dreams, miracles, signs, and wonders.

For years he did not know what to do with the unique experiences, so he just wrote them in his journals. Then, years later, God spoke to him and revealed that he had been chosen as a vessel to point the world to Jesus Christ. So now, he shares fresh revelation from the Spirit of God, the Word of God, and faith-filled testimonies as recorded in his journals.

Following that divine encounter, Gifts of the Holy Spirit began to flow more frequently and with greater clarity within him. Today, thousands have heard him minister the supernatural power of God, with signs and wonders following. As a prophet of God, he teaches and preaches the WORD of God, with revelation, knowledge, and with the demonstration of the power of God. He operates in dreams, visions, prophecy, miracles, signs, and wonders.

Ezekiel spent twelve years in the U.S. Navy and worked as a teacher for fourteen years. He served as an Assistant Pastor for three years at Ceiba Christian Church and then as Senior Pastor for seven years at Resurrection Life Christian Fellowship. He served for several years as an Associate Pastor and Membership Relations Liaison for The Faith Center Ministries under Senior Pastor Bishop Henry Fernandez. He taught as an Associate Professor at the School of the Prophets at the University of Fort Lauderdale.

He has a passion for helping people find their purpose in God and fulfill their destiny in Jesus Christ, through Baptism in the Holy Spirit. He hosts Tuesday World weekly broadcasts, Spiritual Warfare Bootcamp training seminars, and Quarterly Prophetic Prayer Conferences. He has a master's degree in business administration (MBA). He has two daughters: Vannessa and Gabryel. He and his wife, Janice, flow together in life and ministry.

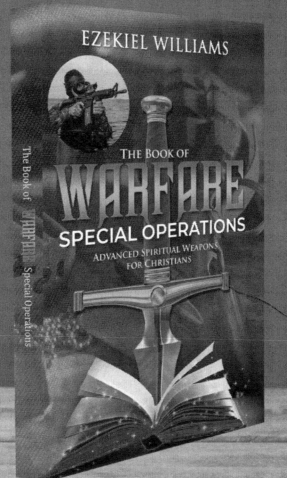

SELECT YOUR LEVEL OF TRAINING
Complete the following challenges and activities to advance in levels.

1a) The Book of Warfare Weapons – Manual

1b) The Book of Warfare Weapons- Social Media Challenge

2) The Book of Warfare Weapons- Workbook

3) The Book of Warfare Weapons- Activities Journal

4) The Book of Warfare Weapons- 8-Hour Audio Training Kit

5) The Book of Warfare- Warriors Group Challenge

6) The Book of Warfare- Outstanding Warriors Challenge (TBOWW-OWC).

7) TBOWW Online Spiritual Warfare Boot Camp.

---

* NOVICE LEVEL-1 Complete activities 1a and 1b.

* BEGINNER LEVEL-2 Completes 1a, 1b, and 2.

* INTERMEDIATE LEVEL-3 Completes 1 through 3.

* JOURNEYMAN-LEVEL-4 Completes 1 through 4.

* ADVANCED LEVEL -5 Completes 1 through 5.

* WARRIOR LEVEL-6 Completes 1 through 6.

* ADVANCED WARRIOR LEVEL-7 Completes 1 to 7.

LEVEL-1

Collect all 50 badges
by completing the
TBOWW Social Media
Challenge

LEVEL-2

**TBOWW
WORKBOOK**

LEVEL-3

**TBOWW
JOURNAL**

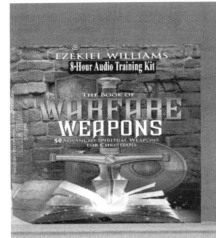

TBOWW 8 HOUR AUDIO TRAINING KIT

LEVEL-4

TBOWW WARRIOR GROUP CHALLENGE

LEVEL-5

TBOWW OUTSTANDING WARRIOR CHALLENGE

LEVEL-6

SPIRITUAL WARFARE
BOOT CAMP
ACTIVATED, EQUIPPED,
AND TRAINED TO WIN

LEVEL-7

INTENSIVE ONLINE

SPIRITUAL WARFARE TRAINING

www.tbowowc.com

How To Best Use The Training Program

The Book of Warfare Weapons (TBOWW) Spiritual Warfare Training program is designed to reach each person where they are and help take them to where they want to go. While the material in the program is designed for Christians, anyone who puts their faith in Jesus Christ can benefit from it.

NOVICE LEVEL-1: Consists of The Book of Warfare Weapons-Manual, and the Social Media Challenge. This is for individuals who want to learn about the 50 different spiritual weapons, how to receive them, activate them, and how to best utilize them. It has a fun social media challenge to challenge your family and friends to take the spiritual warfare journey with you.

BEGINNER LEVEL-2: Consists of The Book of Warfare Weapon-Workbook. The workbook is for individuals who want to learn by doing. It gives you specific activities, challenges, exercises, and ideas to help you put what you have learned into action.

INTERMEDIATE LEVEL-3: Consists of The Book of Warfare Weapons-Journal. This activities Journal is to be utilized in conjunction with the specific activities, challenges, and exercises from the workbook. Completing the journal takes your training to another level and helps you to think critically, develop spiritual reasoning, thought-provoking analysis, and soul-searching reflection on what is presented in the manual and workbook.

JOURNEYMAN LEVEL-4: Consists of The Book of Warfare Weapons- 8-Hour Audio Training Kit. This is 8 hours of spiritual warfare teachings, revelations, testimonies of dreams, visions, miracles, signs, and wonders that will recharge your faith. You will hear real-life testimonies from the author of his personal experiences with the 50 spiritual weapons and some testimonies of others whose testimonies will inspire you.

ADVANCED LEVEL-5: Consists of The Book of Warfare Weapons- Warrior Group Challenge. This is where you get to build your small-group bible study of 10 people. There are a lot of group activities, challenges, and exercises that you and your group can complete together. The activities will help you exercise and practice as a group what you have learned. The exercises are fun but can be very impacting on you, your family, your church, and your community. You can expect to make lasting memories, lifelong experiences, strengthen group bonds, and impact the lives of those around you while having more opportunities to exercise your spiritual weapons. Register for the free training and receive ongoing support to help you get the most out of the TBOWW small-group experience.

WARRIOR LEVEL-6: Consists of The Book of Warfare Outstanding Warriors Challenge. This is where you get to bring together all the information that you have learned on each of the previous levels. This is where you demonstrate your understanding and comprehension of the material in an online eLearning and review platform.   The successful completion of this level is where you can join the ranks of other trained Christian men and women who have become recognized as The Book of Warfare Weapons Outstanding Warriors (TBOWWOW).

ADVANCED WARRIOR LEVEL-7:   Consists of TBOWW Spiritual Warfare Bootcamp. After reaching the Warrior Level, some of you may want to go even further in your training. If you are currently in ministry, desire to be in the future, or you serve in a leadership position in a church or ministry, this training is for you. It is also great training for intercessors, armor bearers, and anyone involved in prophetic, deliverance, and healing ministries. This is an intense online training program that is designed to help activate you to "take ground," in the Name of Jesus Christ. The training will focus on equipping you with additional strategies, tactics, tools, and resources to be successful in spiritual warfare. Individuals who complete the advanced training will also have unique opportunities to participate in special live training and networking events nationally and globally.

VISIT US ON OUR WEBSITES

thebookofwarfare.com

tbowowc.com

tbowwgroups.com

tbowgwn.com

CONNECT WITH US ON SOCIAL MEDIA

YOUTUBE:
tbowowc

FACEBOOK:
tbowowc

INSTAGRAM:
tbowowc

TWITTER:
@tbowowc

Thank you for connecting with us.

TBOW

OUTSTANDING WARRIORS CHALLENGE

RAISING WARRIORS TO WIN

Scan the QR Code below
to begin the challenge.

Made in the USA
Columbia, SC
30 July 2022

64331738R00109